Institute of Leadership
& Management

superseries

Managing the Employment Relationship

FIFTH EDITION

Published for the
Institute of Leadership & Management

ELSEVIER

AMSTERDAM • BOSTON • HEIDELBERG • LONDON • NEW YORK • OXFORD
PARIS • SAN DIEGO • SAN FRANCISCO • SINGAPORE • SYDNEY • TOKYO
Pergamon Flexible Learning is an imprint of Elsevier

Pergamon
Flexible
Learning

Pergamon Flexible Learning is an imprint of Elsevier
Linacre House, Jordan Hill, Oxford OX2 8DP, UK
30 Corporate Drive, Suite 400, Burlington, MA 01803, USA

First edition 1986
Second edition 1991
Third edition 1997
Fourth edition 2003
Fifth edition 2007

Editor: David Pardey

Based on material in previous editions of this work

The views expressed in this work are those of the authors and do
not necessarily reflect those of the Institute of Leadership &
Management or of the publisher

Notice
No responsibility is assumed by the publisher for any injury and/or damage to persons or
property as a matter of products liability, negligence or otherwise, or from any use or operation
of any methods, products, instructions or ideas contained in the material herein

British Library Cataloguing in Publication Data
A catalogue record for this book is available from the British Library

Library of Congress Cataloguing in Publication Data
A catalogue record for this book is available from the Library of Congress

ISBN 978-0-08-046443-5

For information on all Pergamon Flexible Learning publications
visit our website at http://books.elsevier.com

Institute of Leadership & Management
Registered Office
1 Giltspur Street
London
EC1A 9DD
Telephone: 020 7294 2470
www.i-l-m.com
ILM is part of the City & Guilds Group

Typeset by Charon Tec Ltd (A Macmillan Company), Chennai, India
www.charontec.com
Printed and bound in Great Britain

07 08 09 10 11   10 9 8 7 6 5 4 3 2 1

Working together to grow
libraries in developing countries

www.elsevier.com | www.bookaid.org | www.sabre.org

ELSEVIER   BOOK AID
            International   Sabre Foundation

Contents

Contents

Series preface

Whether you are a tutor/trainer or studying management development to further your career, Super Series provides an exciting and flexible resource to help you to achieve your goals. The fifth edition is completely new and up-to-date, and has been structured to perfectly match the Institute of Leadership & Management (ILM)'s new unit-based qualifications for first line managers. It also harmonizes with the 2004 national occupational standards in management and leadership, providing an invaluable resource for S/NVQs at Level 3 in Management.

Super Series is equally valuable for anyone tutoring or studying any management programmes at this level, whether leading to a qualification or not. Individual workbooks also support short programmes, which may be recognized by ILM as Endorsed or Development Awards, or provide the ideal way to undertake CPD activities.

For learners, coping with all the pressures of today's world, Super Series offers you the flexibility to study at your own pace to fit around your professional and other commitments. You don't need a PC or to attend classes at a specific time – choose when and where to study to suit yourself! And you will always have the complete workbook as a quick reference just when you need it.

For tutors/trainers, Super Series provides an invaluable guide to what needs to be covered, and in what depth. It also allows learners who miss occasional sessions to 'catch up' by dipping into the series.

Super Series provides unrivalled support for all those involved in first line management and supervision.

Unit specification

Title:	Managing the employment relationship	Unit Ref:	M3.16
Level:	3		
Credit value:	1		

Learning outcomes *The learner will*	Assessment criteria *The learner can (in an organization with which the learner is familiar)*	
1. Understand diversity in the workplace	1.1	Identify the main provisions of statutory requirements for the employment relationship, discrimination at work and fair employment
	1.2	Identify the organization's employment policies and procedures that could guide the first line manager in managing diversity in the workplace
	1.3	Explain the importance of diversity in the workplace
	1.4	Explain the consequences of non compliance with diversity policies for own work area and for the organization
2. Know how to maintain discipline in the workplace	2.1	Identify the organization's employment policies and procedures that could guide the first line manager in dealing with disciplinary issues
	2.2	Describe how you could monitor discipline in the workplace
	2.3	Briefly describe the legal aspects of the disciplinary process
	2.4	Review own ability to maintain discipline in the workplace

Workbook introduction

1 ILM Super Series study links

This workbook addresses the issues of *Managing the Employment Relationship*. Should you wish to extend your study to other Super Series workbooks covering related or different subject areas, you will find a comprehensive list at the back of this book.

2 Links to ILM qualifications

This workbook relates to the learning outcomes of Unit M3.16 Managing the employment relationship from the ILM Level 3 Award, Certificate and Diploma in First Line Management.

3 Links to S/NVQs in management

This workbook relates to the following Unit of the Management Standards which are used in S/NVQs in Management, as well as a range of other S/NVQs:

B11. Promote diversity in your area of responsibility

4 Workbook objectives

The United Kingdom has always had a population distinguished by its diversity. From prehistoric times invaders have settled here, bringing with them new skills, customs and religious beliefs. Although at the time the incomers were seen as a threat, their arrival was, in fact, beneficial to society as a whole.

Human beings come in a diversity of shapes, sizes, abilities and other characteristics, many of which they have no control over.

However, wherever there is diversity, i.e. where people are different from each other, there is a risk of inequality.

Nowadays just about everyone would agree that equality is a good idea, but too often, it seems, the same groups of people tend to miss out on advantages and opportunities.

As a first line manager, you are responsible for making sure that you make the most of diversity within your team, and that every team member is treated fairly and understands the importance of equality in the workplace.

This workbook discusses the reasons why it is important to protect diversity and avoid inequality and discrimination at work. We will explore methods that you can use to check whether inequality has occurred in your workplace, and find out about the kinds of protection extended to certain groups under the law. It is very important for you, as a manager, to be aware of your responsibilities. Adhering to the law need not be difficult but the penalties for breaking it can be high.

Keeping within the law is one thing, but for a really successful work team a more pro-active approach is usually required. Later parts of this workbook therefore describe the practical steps you can take to develop a culture of equality in your workplace.

Failure to comply with the legislation that protects diversity has serious consequences, both for you and your organization.

For most people, most of the time, no major problems arise, and the formal aspects of management procedures are not the subject of debate. As a first line manager you can contribute to this favourable climate by knowing and implementing your organization's procedures implicitly.

You also need to have an appreciation of the underlying laws that have been developed over many years to provide the minimum standards that every employee, in any working situation, can expect to be applied. The law increasingly influences the way in which employers must frame their policies.

Trades unions came into being in an era when many employers exercised absolute powers over their staff and frequently abused those powers. The unions helped to establish reasonable minimum working conditions for employees. The unions' role has changed over the years, but they still represent the interests of millions of employees in a wide variety of occupations. Dealings with them are an everyday aspect of some first line managers' working lives.

In this workbook, we will look at some aspects of the management policies, procedures and approaches that help to create good working relationships. These are effective for 95% of the time with 95% of employees – and even more in well run organizations.

However, for those employers and employees who cannot, or will not, work within such policies, the law provides a framework that both parties must work within. First line managers need to be aware of that framework and use their skills, training and experience to ensure that the procedures are applied fairly and consistently.

4.1 Objectives

When you have completed this workbook you will be better able to:

■ define 'diversity' and explain why it is important to manage diversity at work;
■ outline the main legislation relating to fair employment;
■ recognize whether the law has been broken;
■ understand and implement your organization's employment policies and procedures as a major step towards managing your team fairly and consistently within the law;
■ describe the steps you can take to ensure diversity in the workplace;
■ describe the consequences of non-compliance for your own work area and organization.
■ deal with disciplinary matters in a fair and consistent way within the law.

5 Activity planner

The following activities require some planning so you may want to look at these now.

- Activity 25, on page 52, which asks you to consider an occasion when you have been involved in a selection process – you should identify ways in which things could have been done differently in order to more effectively ensure equality.
- Activity 29, on page 59, which asks you to obtain a copy of your organization's policy and procedures relating to diversity and equal opportunities.
- Activity 31, on page 63, which asks you to think about practical steps you can take to ensure that members of your work team are treated fairly.
- Activity 32, on page 68, asks you to obtain a copy of your organization's employee or organization handbook.

Either Activity 25 or Activity 31 may provide the basis of evidence for your S/NVQ portfolio. All Portfolio Activities and the Work-based assignment are signposted with this icon.

The icon states the elements to which the Portfolio Activities and Work-based assignment relate.

The Work-based assignment, on page 147, will require that you spend time gathering information and talking to colleagues and people in your work team. You might like to start thinking about whom you should approach, and perhaps arrange a time or chat with them.

Session A
Managing diversity

1 Introduction

Wherever you are in the world, whenever you get a group of people together, you will find that in fact everyone is different – there is diversity. Members of the group may appear to have overwhelmingly similar characteristics, for example all male, all under 20, all European in origin, but if you dig deeper you will find innumerable differences – in physical or mental limitations, sexual orientation, religious beliefs, and so on.

Research has shown that, when people are perceived as being 'different', there is a danger that they can be subject to unequal treatment. Those who have characteristics which other people perceive as 'good' may be treated in a more favourable way than those who have characteristics perceived as 'bad'. One particularly famous piece of research in the USA illustrated this clearly. Researchers carried out an experiment in which a group of college students were required to wear black armbands for a week. Gradually the rest of the student population became less friendly towards them and increasingly discriminated against them without being able to explain why. This research, together with many similar experiments, shows that diversity, i.e. being 'different', carries a risk.

In every organization, and in every work team within that organization, you will find diversity that needs to be managed. It is the first line manager's responsibility to ensure that everyone is treated equally, and that no one is discriminated against because of race, gender, sexual inclination, age, religion, cultural origin, or physical or mental ability.

2 Diversity and equality

Where there is diversity in your work team you are responsible for ensuring that, whatever their characteristics, everyone is treated with equality. The next step is to have a clear idea of what 'equality' means.

Think about the word for a minute or two, then complete the first Activity.

Activity 1

5 mins

Try to think of **two** or **three** alternative definitions for the word 'equality'.

_____

_____

_____

Perhaps you've written something like:

'the same opportunities being open to everyone', or
'everybody being treated the same', or
'everyone being on an equal footing'.

All these, and similar definitions, are perfectly good in a general kind of way but we need to be a little more specific.

Activity 2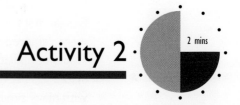

2 mins

Below are two statements about equality. Consider them in relation to the workplace specifically.

Equality means everyone must like one another.
Equality means everybody is equal.

There is a problem with these statements. In the space below note any problems that occur to you as you consider them.

_____

_____

_____

_____

Sadly, each of these definitions is unrealistic and quite impossible to achieve! No manager, however efficient, is able to make people like each other and, for better or worse, we simply are not all equal.

All that equality means is that when there is diversity no one should be treated less favourably than anyone else. So a reasonable definition of inequality would be as follows.

Inequality occurs when a person or group is treated in a less favourable way than another is, or would be, treated in the same sort of situation.

However, there is one important word missing from this definition. Perhaps you have already guessed what it is. In Section 4 of this unit we will be able to define inequality more precisely.

3 The importance of equality at work

What sort of difficulties would you face if people felt there was inequality of treatment in your workplace?

Activity 3 · 4 mins

From your own experience, jot down two problems you would have to deal with.

_____

_____

_____

_____

Typically:

- morale might be low and relationships between members of the work team, and their relationship with you, might suffer;
- the best use might not be made of everybody's diverse abilities;
- there might be high rates of sickness, absenteeism and wastage resulting from people's discouragement with the job;
- there might be conflict leading to lost production – and possibly even strikes;
- there could be the possibility of legal action against the company;
- it is possible that you would be found personally responsible in law for discrimination in the workplace.

I expect that you thought of other difficulties, but this list is probably enough to help us see the practical and legal reasons why achieving equality in a diverse environment is so important for the team leader.

No one likes to feel that they are suffering the disadvantage of being treated unfavourably.

Equality of treatment and opportunity is important:

- to encourage good relationships in the workplace; **and**
- to make the best use of everyone's abilities.

4 Inequality and unfairness at work

Now let us think more carefully about inequality.

As we have seen, inequality is not about people **being** unequal. It is about being **treated** less favourably than others, so that they suffer some disadvantage as a result. When we talk about unfairness, we mean that people are not getting their rights – justice is not being done.

However, inequality is only **one** kind of unfairness. Even if everyone were to be treated equally at work, so that no inequality existed, **other** forms of unfairness could still exist. So we cannot say that inequality at work simply means that someone is being treated unfairly. Inequality is a special kind of unfairness. There is a difference between being unfair to people and treating someone in an unequal way compared to others. You could be consistently unfair to everyone which would still mean that everyone was being treated equally!

Inequality occurs when a person or group is unjustifiably treated in a less favourable way than another is, or would be, treated in the same sort of situation.

This word '**unjustifiably**' is a vital one. After all, however much you may want to treat everyone equally at work, sometimes it is impossible to do so. Often there is some overwhelming reason which prevents you from doing so. Take the following case.

Activity 4

3 mins

> Three young assistants were serving in a butcher's shop. Viv had long and straggling hair. Maria and Karl had short and tidy hair. The manager had repeatedly told Viv that, unless he got his hair cut short, or tied it back neatly while he was in the shop, he could not stay in the job. Viv refused, and finally was dismissed.

The manager had a strong enough justification for his treatment of Viv to make it clear that this was not a case of inequality at work. What do you think the justification was?

_____

_____

You probably, and correctly, put something like: 'hygiene' or 'to ensure that the meat was not exposed to germs' or 'to protect customers from contaminated meat'.

On the face of it, the manager seems to have treated Viv differently from the others, in a way that put Viv at a disadvantage in the end. But his reason for doing so was because of the overwhelming need to ensure good hygiene in a fresh food shop. The manager, incidentally, was able to prove that he had fully explained his reason to Viv, and that no one was ever allowed to serve in the shop who did not meet the defined hygiene standards. This was further proof of the manager's case that his treatment of Viv was justified.

So we can now make the following statements.

■ Inequality occurs when a person or group is unjustifiably treated in a less favourable way than another is, or would be, treated in the same sort of situation.
■ Some inequalities at work cannot be avoided. The essential thing is that, if they exist, there is a strong justification for them.

There is one more important point to make here.

Before making any decision, get the facts.

When you are looking into any complaint, or checking a situation in your workplace, you must get all the important facts before you attempt to make any decisions. This is vital in issues related to equality at work, because such issues have so many legal as well as practical implications.

5 Has inequality occurred? – a checklist

In order that we can decide, in a particular situation, whether inequality of treatment has occurred, there are four crucial questions to be answered.

1   What are the **facts**?

2   Is there any **difference in treatment**?

3   Does anyone suffer any **disadvantage**?

4   Does any **justification** exist?

Let's try out the checklist on another situation.

Activity 5

4 mins

Mr Singh, a Sikh, applied for a job on the production line in a factory manufacturing sweets. As an orthodox Sikh, he wore a beard. He was told he could have the job, providing that he shaved off his beard. His religion forbade him to do this, so he failed to get the job.

What are the facts?

Jot down **four** pieces of information, not given here, in the form of questions that you will need to have answered before being able to decide whether or not Mr Singh has suffered from inequality of treatment.

For example, you might want to know whether the non-wearing of beards was a stated condition of employment.

_____

_____

_____

_____

Your questions may be included in the following list. You may also have thought of other pieces of information you feel you need.

- Is the non-wearing of beards a stated condition of employment?
- Have other bearded applicants been treated in the same way as Mr Singh?
- Is there any other reason why Mr Singh did not get the job, for instance: lack of ability?
- Why was Mr Singh told to shave his beard?
- Are there any rules in the factory about non-wearing of beards by existing workers?
- Do any existing workers wear beards?
- Is there any strong justification for non-wearing of beards in the factory?

Here are the full facts that an investigation into this case actually revealed.

Mr Singh, a Sikh, applied for a job in a factory manufacturing sweets. A factory rule forbade the wearing of beards by any employee who came into contact with the products. This rule was strictly applied to existing workers, and was a condition of employment for new workers.

The application of this rule meant that Sikhs, whose religion forbids them to shave their beards, were virtually ruled out of taking such jobs. However, the employer maintained that the rule was justifiable on grounds of hygiene, irrespective of the colour, race or nationality of applicants and job holders. He was able to show that no one with a beard had ever obtained or kept a job that involved contact with the products.

Mr Singh was fully qualified to do the job, and was offered it. But when told that he must obey the rule and shave his beard off he declined to do so, since he was an orthodox Sikh and could not disobey the rules of his religion.

Activity 6

Now that we know a whole lot more, we can move on to apply the rest of our checklist and answer the following questions.

Is there any **difference in treatment**? Who, if anyone, has received **difference in treatment** in this case?

_____

Did anyone suffer any **disadvantage**? What, if disadvantage has occurred as a result of any difference in treatment?

_____

_____

Does any **justification** exist? What, if any, strong justification exists for any unfavourable treatment?

_____

_____

Now let's look at the answers to these questions.

- Is there any **difference in treatment**?

  Mr Singh was not treated differently from anyone else. The no-beard rule applied to everyone.

- Did anyone suffer any **disadvantage**?

  Mr Singh failed to get the job because he wouldn't shave off his beard. So, yes, he did suffer a disadvantage.

- Does any **justification** exist?

  The justification is hygiene, as in our case about the assistants in the butcher's shop. Hygiene near food products is clearly a very strong justification. The firm was also quite clear about it: no one who worked near food products had ever been allowed to wear a beard. This consistant treatment shows just how important the hygiene factor was.

  So did inequality occur? No – the Employment Tribunal which investigated this case decided that the justification for non-wearing of beards was so strong that no true inequality occurred in this case. Again, let's remember the following.

Inequality occurs when a person or group is unjustifiably treated in a less favourable way than another is, or would be, in the same sort of situation.

Did you notice the way in which our four-point checklist helped us to build up an increasingly clear understanding of all the issues in the case? At the end, we could confidently answer the question 'Did inequality occur here?'

Let's try out our checklist once more.

Activity 7

5 mins

I   What are the **facts**?

> An Afro-Caribbean skilled fitter applied for a job with a large motor manufacturer. He was well qualified for the job, and management wished to appoint him. Both the company and the trade union claimed to actively pursue a policy of equal opportunity for all workers, regardless of colour, race or sex.
>
> All the other workers in the section where the job was located were white. A union meeting was held, and a resolution was passed that the white workers would not work with a black person. The two shop stewards told management, who then decided not to appoint the black applicant. One white worker disagreed with the union action. He reported the firm for inequality at work.

Now try answering the rest of the questions in our checklist.

2   Is there any **difference in treatment**? Who, if anyone, has received difference in treatment?

_____

3   Did anyone suffer any **disadvantage**? What, if any, disadvantage has occurred as a result of any difference in treatment?

_____

_____

4 Does any **justification** exist? What, if any, strong justification exists for any unfavourable treatment?

_____

_____

So has inequality at work occurred here? YES/NO/UNSURE

Let's look at the answers now.

- Certainly the Afro-Caribbean fitter was treated differently from the way any white applicant would have been — although, clearly, any applicant from an ethnic minority would have been treated in the same way as he was.
- The fitter definitely suffered a disadvantage, in that he did not get the job.
- Was there strong justification for such unfavourable treatment? Questions of justifiability are not always easy to answer; you may have found this one difficult. The virtual certainty of management facing a strike if they employed the black fitter might be seen as a compelling reason for not employing him.

But let's consider the other side of the story.

There was an active equal opportunity policy in the firm, to which management and union were both committed. They had agreed to apply this policy regardless of colour and so on. So to reject a person simply on grounds of colour went right against this policy.

Can such a rejection simply on grounds of ethnic origin ever be justifiable? Our own society condemns racism. Surely such a rejection encourages racism, and will lead to more inequality in that firm?

To reject a black person because of threats from white workers could be seen as giving in to unreasonable demands.

In fact the Commission for Racial Equality, who considered the case, decided that the firm had no justification for the treatment of the fitter. They decided that it was a case of inequality at work.

We will come back to this case later, because for several other reasons it is an important one in relation to inequality. For the moment, though, we can see again how our four-point checklist helps us to build up an increasingly clear understanding of all the issues in a case until, at the end, we can answer the following question with reasonable confidence.

'Did inequality occur here?'

Self-assessment 1

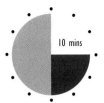

10 mins

1   Give five reasons why someone might be discriminated against in the workplace.

2   Fill in the blanks in the sentences with a suitable word or words.

   Equality of treatment and _____ is important:

   ■ to encourage good _____ in the workplace; and

   ■ to make the best use of everyone's _____.

3   Inequality occurs when a person or _____ is _____ treated in a less _____ way than another is, or would be, treated in the same sort of situation.

4   The four-point checklist.

   a What are the _____?

   b Is there any difference in _____?

   c Does anyone suffer any _____?

   d Does any _____ exist?

5   One of the following four statements is false; the rest are true. Try to identify the false statement.

   ■ Equality means everyone has the same abilities and opportunities.   ❒

   ■ Inequality exists when a group is unjustifiably treated differently from another group.   ❒

   ■ Inequality of treatment may lead to low morale and conflict in the workplace.   ❒

   ■ A manager can be found personally responsible in law for inequality in the workplace.   ❒

Answers to these questions can be found on pages 162–3.

6 Summary

- **Diversity** is the mix of cultures, ethnic background, religion, sex and other personal characteristics found in the workplace.

- Diversity has to be **managed** in order to avoid unfair discrimination and inequality of treatment.

- Equality of treatment and opportunity encourages good relations at work and makes the best use of everyone's abilities.

- **Inequality occurs when a person or group is unjustifiably treated in a less favourable way than another is, or would be, treated in the same sort of situation.**

- If inequalities occur there must be strong justification for them.

- Four-point checklist.

    - What are the **facts**?
    - Is there any **difference** in **treatment**?
    - Does anyone suffer any **disadvantage**?
    - Does any **justification** exist?

Session B
The law relating to equality at work

1 Introduction

The law has intervened increasingly in recent years to regulate relationships between employers and employees. It is a complicated area and in a continuing state of flux. Though the basic Acts do not change much, subsequent 'Directives' and the huge numbers of decisions taken by employment tribunals and the courts affect the law in subtle, and sometimes radical, ways. There can never be a definitive statement of the law, and so the best way to keep within it is to manage within the spirit of it, so demonstrating your commitment to equality in practice.

1.1 Changing trends

Changing the law does not of itself alter prejudices. They may be deeply rooted and will change only, if ever, over extended periods of time. However, such changes **have** occurred in areas touched on by the law. Tasks once almost exclusively undertaken by men, such as dentistry, engineering, flying aircraft and driving heavy goods vehicles are now much more commonly performed by women. Statistics published in 2002 indicate that since 1951:

- the proportion of women in the UK workforce has increased from 30% to 45%;
- the proportion of women managers has increased from 15% to 30%;
- the proportion of women in professional occupations has risen from 8% to 42%.

1.2 Unchanging attitudes

It would be hard to find a single human being who is totally without prejudice, even if it is simply in regard to what is, or is not, a suitable job to apply for, and even where no physical barrier to doing the job exists.

Changing the law cannot make people apply for jobs which they believe are traditionally not done by members of their own sex or ethnic group. There may also be pressures inside their own communities which inhibit them, for example Roman Catholics in Northern Ireland or West Indians in London may be reluctant to join the police force.

1.3 Modifying behaviour

The law cannot remove people's prejudices about those who do not look, speak, behave or believe as they do. Whether their reasons are rational or irrational they are quite beyond the ability of the law to change.

What the law **can** do is to insist that people's behaviour conforms to certain standards. Statute law is enforced by sanctions available through the courts and employment tribunals, before which people who believe that they have been discriminated against illegally can have their cases heard.

In a parliamentary democracy, over a period of time, laws will reflect what the majority of people recognize as being just and fair. In the nineteenth century, that included flogging in the army, navy and prisons, transportation for life for many offences, and the outlawing of trade union activity under the combination laws. All of these laws changed as general public opinion moved against them. No doubt some people regretted the changes, but they had to learn to live with them.

Likewise, individuals who disagree with laws outlawing discrimination in specified circumstances must obey them in public, whatever they may think in private.

1.4 Diversity

Over the centuries the UK has welcomed and absorbed people from many countries for many reasons. They add to the variety of skills and experiences available here by comparison with societies where such inflows of people have not happened.

The concept of 'managing diversity' has already been discussed in Session A. Managing diversity implies:

- recognizing and drawing out the contributions which all individuals have to offer through their differing backgrounds, experiences, cultures and inclinations;
- melding them to produce a total effort whose sum is greater than the sum of its parts.

If, as a first line manager, you apply such an approach to your everyday duties then you will be going a long way towards meeting the positive intentions of the various laws you will be looking at in this session.

Activity 8 · 3 mins

Imagine yourself managing a team of 12 people consisting of individuals from both sexes, of various ages, from four identifiable ethnic backgrounds and two religions. One member is physically disabled. List up to four advantages which such a team would have over one which comprised members of a single sex, ethnic group, age group and physical ability level.

_____

_____

_____

_____

This Activity has asked you to consider the positive aspects of managing a diverse team. The factors which you listed could include the following.

- A disabled person has experience of and sympathy with disabled customers who use your products or have to negotiate entrances and changes in floor level on your premises.
- People from different religions can anticipate sensibilities which may affect the marketability of particular products or services to members of their faiths.
- Younger people may have greater enthusiasm, sharper physical reactions and willingness to look at different ways of doing things.
- Men and women can bring complementary views to bear on opportunities or problems in the design of products.
- Experienced staff may be less prone to panic when things don't go according to plan and have solutions available which they know work.
- People from different cultures may bring ideas which are more sensitive to environmental issues, avoiding waste and working harmoniously with the environment.

You may have other ideas, but in principle the Activity should help you think positively about managing diverse teams and the honourable intentions underlying the legislation.

2 Scope of the anti-discrimination laws

The law does not impose a blanket ban on discrimination for any and every reason. For example, it does not demand that all jobs be filled on a 'first come first appointed' basis or insist that untrained people be allowed to work as surgeons, airline pilots, teachers or food handlers.

However, the law does aim to outlaw unfair discrimination against anyone on the following well-defined grounds:

In 2002 a Roman Catholic man was awarded £10,000 by the European Court of Human Rights in Strasbourg. It upheld his claim that he had been discriminated against because of his 'religious belief or political opinion' when dismissed from his job as a waiter by a hotel in Belfast. He stated that he had been the only Catholic among the staff.

- sex;
- marital status;
- race;
- colour;
- nationality;
- ethnic origin;
- national origin;
- disability;
- age;
- sexual orientation (homosexuality, heterosexuality or bisexuality);
- religion or belief.

2.1 Positive discrimination

The law does not require general discrimination **in favour of** particular groups or individuals except under well-defined circumstances.

There has been much debate about having all-women lists as candidates for parliamentary seats in order to increase representation by women in the House of Commons and the Government. But positive sex discrimination is not treated as a general principle by the law as it currently stands.

Activity 9

Why do you think that the legislators have fought shy of demanding more general positive discrimination throughout the working population? Try to make three suggestions.

_____

_____

_____

You may have thought of a number of reasons, including the following.

- People might actually feel patronized and be reluctant to be appointed into jobs simply because they are from one of the groups mentioned. 'Tokenism' can offend the person who is selected to be the 'token', as well as everyone else working in that area.
- There may be underlying causes concerning education and training which need to be eliminated – positive discrimination alone would not address these issues.
- Discriminating in favour of one group could discriminate against another group, which the law is also seeking to protect.
- Unless the person appointed is competent, there could be repercussions concerning general standards of work, safety, employment relations and commercial viability.

2.2 Genuine Occupational Qualification (GOQ)

The law does provide for an employer to claim that discrimination was necessary because of a 'genuine occupational qualification (GOQ)'. For example, many jobs demand that their holders fulfil requirements relating to such matters as taste, decency, artistic credibility and the sensibilities of various defined groups.

Activity 10

3 mins

Look at the following list of job advertisements and underline those in which you believe an employer could validly argue that a GOQ existed which would disqualify any applicants who did not possess it.

1 Packing machine operator

2 Gentleman's cloakroom attendant

3 Catering assistant

4 Dancer to play Juliet in Prokofiev's 'Romeo and Juliet' ballet

5 Sailor to work on Scottish Islands ferry services

6 Waiter/waitress for Chinese restaurant

7 Actor to play Hamlet, Prince of Denmark (Shakespeare)

8 Nurse for maternity hospital

9 Front line infantry soldiers

10 Santa Claus for Christmas season in department store

Of the ten jobs listed, five clearly cannot claim a credible GOQ.

In job 1, there is no GOQ because someone from any race, either sex and many disabled people could do the job. The same applies to job 3. In job 5, a sailor does not have to be Scottish or from any particular race to work on such a ferry. In job 8, men work as gynaecologists and as midwives, so there is no GOQ to prevent their working in a maternity hospital. As far as job 10 is concerned, Santa Claus, with voluminous costume and false beard, could be played by either sex – though no test case has yet come to tribunal, so far as is known.

You could have underlined five jobs, but even some of these could be contentious.

A singer applied for the role of a virgin in a Gilbert and Sullivan opera. She was clearly expecting a child and was turned down. Backed by her union, she took her case to a tribunal, claiming unfair discrimination. She lost the case on the grounds that there was a GOQ and her condition clearly made her ineligible for authenticity in the role.

In job 2, it could be argued that on grounds of privacy and decency only a male could do this job in such intimate surroundings – but since men work as nurses in female wards there could be a counter-argument.

In job 4, it is difficult to see how a male dancer, however good, could play this role in a normal production – but there have been all-male performances of 'Swan Lake'.

In job 6, it could be held that only somebody authentically Chinese could do the job, but would the same be true for a restaurant promoting authentic French, Italian or English Food?

In regard to job 7, Hamlet is a role written for a man, but it has been played in the past by some famous actresses, including Sarah Bernhardt, who had also lost one leg by the time she played it.

The situation in job 9 has now been clarified. After long debate, the Ministry of Defence has concluded that only men possess the necessary attributes to serve in front line combat situations.

As you will have seen, even in the underlined situations, there is some room for debate. Discussion still continues about women's suitability for hand-to-hand combat roles and their effect on morale and discipline in front line infantry formations. Often, the issues are not clear cut.

3 United Kingdom statute law

Normally, statute law enacted by Parliament is enforceable by the courts or other bodies empowered to do so under a specific Act.

Under European Union (EU) law, there are some matters in which UK statute law does not take precedence. Some actual or proposed European Directives will be covered later on.

Under UK law there are a number of principal statutes relating to the unfair forms of discrimination so far declared illegal. These are as follows.

EXTENSION I summarizes the work of the Equal Opportunities Commission (EOC), the Commission for Racial Equality (CRE) and the Disability Rights Commission (DRC)

The Sex Discrimination Acts of 1975 and 1986
These prohibit unfair discrimination on grounds relating to sex or marital status.

The Employment Protection (Consolidation) Act 1978, the Employment Act 1980 and the Social Security Act 1986
These give pregnant employees, or those on (or returning from) maternity leave certain rights relating to pay and jobs.

The Equal Pay Act 1970, amended in 1983
This requires that men and women in a particular workplace receive equal pay for work which is the same or similar, and for work of equal value.

The Race Relations Act of 1976
This prohibits unfair discrimination on grounds relating to race or nationality.

The Disability Discrimination Act 1995
This prohibits unfair discrimination on grounds relating to disability.

Employment Act 2002
This gives women returning to work after childbirth the right to request part-time employment but a woman exercising this right should normally exhaust all internal procedures before taking this to an Employment Tribunal.

Employment Equality (Sexual Orientation) Regulations 2003
This prohibits discrimination on the grounds of someone's sexual orientation.

Employment Equality (Religion or Belief) Regulations 2003
This prohibits discrimination on the grounds of perceived as well as their actual religion or belief.

The Employment Equality (Age) Regulations 2006
This prohibits discrimination on the grounds of someone's age.

There are often a number of Amendments to Acts. Those quoted above are selected on the basis of their relevance here.

3.1 Are there ways around the law?

No one can legally enter into a contract which ignores or sets aside statute law, even if both parties agree to it.

Activity 11

A male nurse discovered that he was being paid less than female colleagues for doing the same job. When he enquired why, he was told that lower rates of pay had been offered to applicants who had been engaged later than the nurses receiving higher pay. He had signed his contract freely and must work for the rate he had agreed. He discovered that a female nurse was receiving the higher rate even though she had started later than he had. He eventually pursued his case at an Employment Tribunal. Do you think the Tribunal found for or against him?

FOR/AGAINST

In fact, the Tribunal found in his favour and awarded him a substantial sum, payable by his employer, to compensate him for lost earnings. This real case clearly shows the following.

1 Employees cannot be bound by a contract which breaks the law, even if they agreed to its terms willingly

2 The legislation applies to both men and women.

3.2 Legally unqualified workers

Some people are unqualified, in a **legal** sense, to work at all. Categories which come within the legal definition as 'unqualified' for any employment are:

■ illegal immigrants;
■ people claiming benefit;
■ children still of compulsory school age.

You are most likely to come into contact with them if you work in certain sectors, such as agriculture, horticulture and hospitality. Such people may seem attractive to employers as being unable to assert any rights and potentially willing to work for low pay.

If you find that someone from such a category has joined your team then:

■ your employer is breaking the law;
■ you should discuss it with your employer and endeavour to have the practice ended.

If you do nothing, you have become a party to it and in effect are breaking the law yourself.

So far this section has introduced much wide-ranging legislation that can affect many aspects of your work. It is a daunting array even to practising lawyers, and it would be quite unrealistic to expect you to become an expert in legislation which changes frequently, can be added to by other Acts and Directives, and is subject to interpretation in various courts.

In English law, ignorance of the law is not a valid defence, which though true, probably doesn't sound very helpful. This means that the sensible approach for you to take to protect yourself from possible repercussions is as follows.

The specific grounds on which discrimination can be unlawful are as follows.

■ Sex
■ Nationality
■ Marital status
■ Ethnic origin
■ Race
■ National origin
■ Colour
■ Disability
■ Age
■ Sexual orientation
■ Religion or belief

1 Keep in mind the broad principles and aims of the law and the specific grounds on which illegal discrimination can occur.

2 Seek advice from your manager or the personnel (or human resource) department if you are ever unsure whether an existing, or proposed, practice may offend the law.

Other sources of information and advice are provided on page 156 of this workbook.

4 Other legislation affecting unfair discrimination

There are a number of other Acts and Directives which affect or will affect, directly or indirectly, discrimination in employment. Often their implications cannot be known until test cases have been decided in the courts, and this can take months or even years.

4.1 Human Rights Act 1998

The Act makes the rights and freedoms that people in the UK enjoy under the European Convention on Human Rights (the Convention) into law, so that they can be enforced by UK courts rather than needing to be appealed to the European Court of Human Rights. These are the right:

- to life;
- not to be subjected to torture or to inhuman or degrading treatment or punishment;
- not to be held in slavery or servitude or perform forced or compulsory labour;
- to liberty and security of person;
- to a fair and public hearing within a reasonable time by an independent and impartial tribunal established by law;
- not to be held guilty of any criminal offence on account of any act or omission which did not constitute a criminal offence under national or international law at the time when it was committed;
- to respect for private and family life, home and correspondence;
- to freedom of thought, conscience and religion;
- to freedom of expression;
- to freedom of peaceful assembly and to freedom of association with others;
- to marry and to found a family, according to the national laws.

The Act also says that 'enjoyment of the rights and freedoms set forth in the Convention shall be secured without discrimination on any ground such as sex, race, colour, language, religion, political or other opinion, national or social origin, association with a national minority, property, birth or other status.

4.2 Parental leave

The right of parents of either sex to take leave, paid or unpaid, can obviously affect equality if, for example, employers are more reluctant to grant it to fathers. More fathers are claiming this as their right.

4.3 Flexible working hours scheme

The entitlement of parents from April 2003 to request more flexible 'family friendly' working practices has further implications for sex discrimination, for example in cases where male parents could be held to have been treated less favourably than female parents. Each case must be looked at on its merits, but if you are handling a request to work more flexibly, it is worth keeping in mind the following Employment Tribunal settlement involving a male car mechanic.

> When a female employee came to the end of six months maternity leave from her employer, her husband asked his own employer to reduce his hours so that he could take his turn in looking after the baby. It seemed a sensible arrangement since his wife's job paid better than his. He was refused his request, being told it would be 'too messy' to arrange. Four female employees in the same company had been granted similar requests. The husband resigned and applied to a Tribunal, alleging sex discrimination. He won his case and £3,600 in compensation on the grounds that the employer would probably have acceded to his request had he been a woman. He had clearly received less favourable treatment as a man. The husband was supported by the Equal Opportunities Commission in what they believed was the first (but probably not the last) case of its kind.

4.4 Working Time Directive

This Directive limits the hours which an employee can normally be **required** to work. Normally the limit is no more than 48 hours a week, or eight hours per night shift, though employees can work longer hours by mutual consent.

Employees in the UK tend to work longer hours than those in other European countries, so the pressure to conform with the maximum periods may increase. If one sex works more hours on average than the other, it is possible that sex discrimination might be claimed to support a reduction.

4.5 Minimum wage legislation

The legal minimum hourly rate payable is increased from time to time, so it is not possible to quote a definitive figure here. If you work in a sector which has relatively low paid staff you should check with your manager or the human resources department what the present level is.

All employers must pay at least the minimum rate per hour as set by the law. However, in employment where 'piece work' is the normal practice – that is payment relates to the number of items produced – they must pay a rate which is at least equal to the minimum wage. So, for example, it would be illegal to set a pace of work which made it impossible for the worker to achieve a payment rate per hour equivalent to the minimum wage.

The minimum wage could have serious legal implications in organizations where women do a high proportion of the low-paid jobs on a piece work basis, while men do a comparable job at a higher rate not based on piece work.

4.6 Contingency planning

The problem for you as a first line manager is to anticipate how these actual or proposed Directives **might** affect illegal discrimination at your workplace. You might consider putting contingency plans in place and making sure that you manage within the spirit of the existing law and best practice, which will create the right climate to absorb further legislation if and when it comes.

The next activity will ask you to think about such contingencies.

Activity 12

Try to think of at least one example (preferably from your own experience) where the following Directives could have been relevant in regard to unfair discrimination.

Directive	Example
1 Human Rights	
2 Working Time	
3 Minimum Wage	
4 Ageism	

You will probably have had to think quite hard over this activity. It will be interesting for you to see how your suggestions compare with those given on page 168. They may depend on the sector you work in and the working practices which exist, and may have existed for many years.

This whole area is one in which you need to be constantly on your guard. You would be well advised to review the employment practices in your department and try to anticipate any which may fall foul of existing or proposed legislation.

4.7 The Public Interest Disclosure Act (PIDA)

This UK statute, the 'Whistleblowing Act', gives protection from victimization to employees who raise a wide range of concerns in regard to working practices in their workplace. The concern does not have to be a personal one – it can refer to another individual or a group of employees whom the 'whistleblower' believes are being treated unfairly.

The Act is often referred to by its nickname because it encourages employees to 'blow the whistle' on employers whom they believe to be breaching the law, or trying to cover up such a breach.

Many situations envisaged by the Act are to do with unfair discrimination issues, such as equal pay, terms and conditions of employment, recruitment and selection, and minimum pay.

The Act protects any employee who raises a genuine concern provided that they have an honest and reasonable suspicion that malpractice has occurred, even though it may transpire later that the concern was unfounded.

> A doctor who was dismissed for 'whistleblowing' over her concerns about patient safety won her case against her former employer. She had been offered £85,000 to drop her case, but refused. The case has so far cost £350,000 in legal fees.

Activity 13   5 mins

Look back for a moment at 3.2 *Legally unqualified workers* in this session.

Imagine yourself working for a business which you suspect of employing male staff from one of the proscribed categories. You have raised the issue with your employer but were fobbed off and, in effect, told to mind your own business. You believe that the staff involved are working for less than the minimum wage and are denying employment to legally qualified female workers who did the job previously.

How might PIDA help you if you are still unsatisfied?

_____

_____

_____

_____

You may have written that, once you were sure that you had exhausted all available internal channels, you could report your concerns to a body such as the Equal Opportunities Commission (EOC). A local solicitor who offers free initial consultations or the Citizen's Advice Bureau would be a prudent first port of call.

5 A detailed look at the main UK legislation

The remainder of this session will take a more detailed look at the principal statutes and the specific forms of unfair discrimination which are outlawed by them.

5.1 The Sex Discrimination Acts and Sex Discrimination (Northern Ireland) Order 1976 of 1975 and 1986

The Act makes unfair discrimination unlawful in full-time and part-time employment and in training. Discrimination against married people because they are married is also dealt with.

The chief matters which the act covers are:

- recruitment and selection for employment;
- appraisals, opportunities for training and promotion;
- dismissal;
- victimization.

5.2 The Employment Protection (Consolidation) Act 1978, the Employment Act 1980 and the Social Security Act 1986

Some specific rights relating to pregnancy and employment are included in these Acts, including:

■ time off for ante-natal care;
■ statutory maternity pay;
■ return to work after maternity leave;
■ protection from dismissal on the grounds of pregnancy.

5.3 The Equal Pay Act 1970 and the Equal Pay Act (Northern Ireland) 1970, amended in 1983

This Act established the right for men and women to receive equal pay for doing the same work – something which, for many years prior to the Act, had not been the custom in some trades where women were frequently paid less than men. The Act applies to part-time as well as full-time employees.

The Act also provides that, where men and women are doing **different** work, they should receive equal pay if an assessment of the total effort, skill and responsibility required for the jobs is the same.

A good way of avoiding the risk of making decisions based on prejudices or subjective criteria is to use objective, recognized job evaluation procedures.

5.4 The Race Relations Act 1976 and Race Relations (Northern Ireland) Order 1997

The Act's main provisions are similar to those in the Sex Discrimination Act, outlawing unfair discrimination concerning:

■ recruitment and selection for employment;
■ appraisals, opportunities for training and promotion;

■ dismissal;
■ victimization.

The Act allows for limited permitted discrimination in those circumstances:

■ where there is a 'GOQ', such as the need to use an artistic or photographic model of the same race as the subject being depicted;
■ where a job is to be done wholly outside Great Britain;
■ where there is the need for special training to meet the needs of a racial group which is under-represented in a specified occupation.

5.5 The Disability Discrimination Act 1995

Employers employing fewer than 15 employees are exempt from the Act. (Before December 1998 the minimum number had been 20.)

The Act defines disability as 'a physical or mental impairment which has a substantial and long term adverse effect on the person's ability to carry out normal day-to-day activities.'

A **temporary** incapacity due, for example, to a sporting accident would not qualify anyone for protection under this Act. Normally the effect must last for 12 months or more.

EXTENSION 2
The Disability Discrimination Act 1995 – What Employers Need to Know is available free from the Disability Rights Commission. Reference is made to possible financial help for physical adjustments to the workplace.

The former quota system which you may have come across was abolished in 1996 with the advent of the more general requirement not to discriminate against disabled people as defined by the new Act. Green Card holders under the former legislation automatically gained the protection provided by the 1995 Act.

In some respects, this Act is more far-reaching in its scope than other legislation as it can require changes to an employer's premises as well as to working practices.

Reasonable adjustments

The Act envisages that employers should make 'reasonable adjustments' to working practices and their premises with the intention of levelling the playing field for disabled people. Some adjustments might be relatively inexpensive, for example providing information in Braille or modifying an office layout to provide more room to manoeuvre wheelchairs.

Financing physical adjustments

Where more substantial expense is involved, such as the installation of ramps, lifts, new access or emergency egress provisions, each case then needs to be looked at on its merits. The analysis should take into account the benefits which the employer will receive because of the employee's combination of skills and experience as well as the costs. For example, an existing employee who becomes disabled may be so valuable to the organization that relatively large outlay is justifiable. The total resources of the organization can be taken into account (not just those of a particular site) when assessing what it is reasonable for it to spend, and the smallest employers are of course exempt from the Act.

In some cases, financial help may be available from the government or a voluntary body involved in helping those who suffer the particular disability involved.

Activity 14

Fill in the blanks in the following sentences.

1   The Sex Discrimination and Race Relations Act both outlaw unfair discrimination on the grounds of _____ and _____ for employment.

2   Under the Disability Discrimination Act, an employee who suffered a _____ incapacity following a skiing accident would _____ be protected.

3   Under the Equal Pay Act, _____ and _____ must be paid _____ for doing the _____ work or work assessed as being of _____ value.

4   It is illegal to dismiss a _____ employee solely on the grounds of pregnancy.

5   Victimization is banned under both the _____ Act and the _____ Act.

6   Disability is defined as a _____ or _____ impairment which has a _____ and long-term _____ effect.

7   Time off for _____ care is a legal right for a pregnant employee as is _____ to _____ after maternity leave.

Answers to the Activity can be found on pages 168–9.

6 Illegal discrimination in detail

The various Acts have much in common in the way that they tackle unfair discrimination.

6.1 Direct discrimination

This occurs when an individual is treated less favourably than another would be treated in the same or similar circumstances on any of the grounds proscribed (disability, sex, marital status, race, colour, nationality, ethnic or national origins).

Activity 15 · 3 mins

A woman claimed unfair discrimination on the grounds of marriage. She worked for the same manager as her husband. The manager did not 'get on' with her husband. She claimed that the manager effectively demoted her out of spite. She was backed by her union.

Read the following sentences and decide whether each of the activities described would constitute direct discrimination.

1   An employer advertises a job in a local newspaper specifying that the requirement is for a 'strong, able-bodied man'. YES/NO

2   A store implements a policy of having only male attendants in the gentlemens' cloakroom and female ones to look after the ladies' restroom.

YES/NO

3   A team leader responsible for interviewing job applicants turns down an applicant who is of Punjabi origin because no one of that extraction currently works in the section. She fears the applicant would not fit in.

YES/NO

4   An employer has an unwritten rule that young married women are never promoted beyond a specified management grade because of concern that family commitments might interfere with their work. YES/NO

5   An overseas employer advertises for a 'male engineer' to work in a predominately Muslim state in Africa. YES/NO

1   This is clearly direct discrimination against women and disabled people and would be illegal.

2   This is a 'genuine occupational qualification' on the grounds of privacy and decency. The store's policy is even-handed between men and women and it could not reasonably be claimed as direct discrimination if, for example, a man applied for a job in the ladies' room.

3   This would be direct discrimination, and the team leader could be held personally responsible in law if acting on his or her own initiative. (The consequences for organizations and individuals will be developed in Session D.)

4   This would be direct discrimination on the grounds of sex and marital status and so illegal. If and when 'ageism' becomes illegal, it could also fall foul of that. The courts will then have to decide what is meant by 'young'.

5   This would not be discrimination as there is provision in the Act, where work is being done wholly outside Great Britain, to take account of local customs and practices where the work is to be done.

6.2 Indirect discrimination

Indirect discrimination occurs when a requirement or condition of employment is applied equally to all groups **but**:

- the condition makes it harder for members of a particular group to comply, and;
- it is entirely irrelevant to their ability to do the job.

Imposing such a condition may simply be a roundabout way of discriminating against a particular group, and that is why it is illegal. For example, imposing a condition that all applicants must be six feet tall or above would plainly discriminate against more women than men, and adding that they should also weigh at least 14 stone would add further to the difficulty for female applicants to comply with the condition.

Not all cases of indirect discrimination may be so clear cut, and the following Activity asks you to look at a number of circumstances and decide whether you believe them to represent 'indirect discrimination'.

Note: earlier versions of the Act did not cover 'indirect' discrimination, and the offence was introduced to stop people who were circumventing the law in ways which the original legislators had not anticipated.

Activity 16

Read the following sentences and decide whether each of the activities described would constitute indirect discrimination.

1   A company's policy decreed that no one was eligible for promotion above a certain grade unless they had ten years' continuous service. A female employee applied for such a post. She had been with them for 12 years, but had left for one year to look after her baby before returning.   YES/NO

2   A company started its annual appraisal system at Grade 3 and made decisions about promotion and skills training on the basis of it. Very few of its staff of Asian or Afro-Caribbean origin worked at these grades.   YES/NO

3   A job advertisement stated that applicants must be chartered members of a specified engineering institute to be considered for the post.   YES/NO

4   An internal company job advertisement stated that applicants must be fluent in written and spoken English.   YES/NO

5   A team leader allocated overtime on the basis that staff working 'after hours' must be capable of reaching an emergency exit in less than two minutes.   YES/NO

6   Opportunities were offered in a horse racing stable to 'staff able to ride proficiently at a weight of less than eight stones'.   YES/NO

You will have needed to think hard about some of these questions. The answers are as follows.

1   This would be indirect discrimination against women, who are more likely to have interrupted service through bearing and raising children, **unless** the company could prove that its rule was vital, which is unlikely. Why not nine years, or twelve years?

2   This practice would bear disproportionately on employees of Asian or Afro-Caribbean origin and so is a form of indirect discrimination.

3   This requirement would not be discriminatory provided that it is a genuine occupational requirement for the work to be done.

4   This could be indirect discrimination if fluent English was not a true requirement of the job, assuming that there were native English speakers within the workforce.

5   Although this practice could indirectly discriminate against disabled employees, it may have been introduced with safety in mind. Nevertheless, it could be illegal discrimination.

6   It is essential for riders in such establishments to be 'lightweights'. The requirement (if applied to both sexes and all ethnic groups) would not discriminate indirectly against any particular group since relatively few members of any of them would be able to meet the two essential requirements.

This Activity should have made you realize that you may need to look hard at existing or proposed practices in your own workplace to check whether they could be interpreted as illegal indirect discrimination.

6.3 Victimization

'Victimization' has a specific meaning under discrimination laws. To claim under them that you have been victimized, you must be able to demonstrate that you have been given less favourable treatment because:

- you have brought proceedings under the law;
- you have given evidence or alleged that discrimination has occurred.

Activity 17

3 mins

Give two examples of possible evidence of victimization under the anti-discrimination laws. One example might be that a supposed 'informant' was passed over for promotion.

_____

_____

Examples you may have chosen might include being:

- assigned to less favourable or less rewarding work;
- chosen for redundancy unfairly ahead of other employees;
- denied opportunities for training;
- disciplined without due cause;
- 'sent to Coventry' by work mates;
- dropped by union members from being a shop steward or safety representative.

6.4 Pressure to discriminate

Under the Disability Discrimination Act, pressure to discriminate only becomes illegal if the discrimination sought actually happens. Nonetheless, the pressure itself is contrary to the spirit of the Act.

This occurs when an individual or a group of people put pressure on another to discriminate. For example, a group of established male employees might 'lean' on their team leader either not to engage female applicants who had applied for a job, or to help freeze them out.

Activity 18 · 3 mins

Can you think of two other ways in which pressure to discriminate might happen?

_____

_____

Examples could include the following.

1 Members of a trade union objecting to working with an individual, possibly backed up with the threat of strike action – possibly in defiance of their own union's policy.

2 An influential long-serving or charismatic individual trying to keep out individuals from a group against which he has a grudge or prejudice for any reason.

3 Members of any ethnic group who have worked together for a long time refusing to work with anyone from a different background.

4 A group of managers of one sex trying to prevent a manager of the other sex intruding into their cosy grouping.

Whatever the reason may be, pressure to discriminate is illegal under the race and sex discrimination laws and can pose a real problem to management at every level, especially if there is a threat of industrial action to back it up, or a more subtle withdrawal of co-operation which might threaten the business.

6.5 Instruction to discriminate

Session D will examine the legal implications for managers at any level who obey an illegal instruction.

Managers are forbidden to order their subordinates or service departments (such as personnel) to follow discriminatory practices. Unfortunately, while illegal instructions might be in writing, they are more likely to be verbal, so they are more difficult to prove. Either way, such instructions are illegal and both the giver of the instruction and any subordinate who obeys it can be in trouble with the law.

An 'instruction to discriminate' can only be given by a person who is in a position of authority over the person instructed, as by a manager to a subordinate. If it came from an equal, a subordinate or someone from another area of the organization, the offence would be 'pressure to discriminate'.

Activity 19 · 3 mins

Read through the following three incidents and state whether each one is an example of (1) pressure to discriminate or (2) instruction to discriminate.

1   The general manager of an organization wrote to the human resources department stating that new apprentices should be recruited only from the children of existing skilled employees, who were predominately of Welsh extraction.

PRESSURE TO DISCRIMINATE ☐   INSTRUCTION TO DISCRIMINATE ☐

2   A team leader was approached by a senior manager from another department who asked him not to recommend any further employees of Asian background to her section as she 'had too many already'.

PRESSURE TO DISCRIMINATE ☐   INSTRUCTION TO DISCRIMINATE ☐

3   At a team meeting, the departmental manager said 'off the record' that he would rather no more female employees were offered training as fork lift truck drivers, as they were creating some bad feeling amongst the long-established male employees.

PRESSURE TO DISCRIMINATE ☐   INSTRUCTION TO DISCRIMINATE ☐

You most probably decided the following.

Incident 1 was a clear instruction to discriminate.

Incident 2 was pressure to discriminate. Though the manager was senior to the team leader, she had no direct authority over him and so could only use influence (or 'pressure'). If she had been speaking to her own subordinates, it would have amounted to an instruction to discriminate, even though the remark was 'off the record' and probably not confirmed in writing.

In incident 3, although the remark was 'off the record' and phrased as a 'request', it was effectively an instruction to discriminate given by a manager to direct subordinates.

Illegal discrimination can be applied in a variety of ways. Knowing what the law demands may make prejudiced people try to get round it in subtle ways, using nods and winks which they know will be taken as instructions but for which no written **evidence** can be found. A practice that is 'suggested' may flout the organization's own equal opportunities policy and reflect individual, rather than organizational, bias.

You do need to be wary of such informal policies as well as the more overt ones for, in law, you could be guilty of an offence for following an instruction which is illegal.

6.6 Segregation

This is a word which has bad connotations in areas such as education and housing in the southern states of America and in South Africa. The practice is generally illegal, though not covered specifically for disabled employees in the Disability Discrimination Act.

It may even arise from good intentions, where a manager decides to assign all employees of one ethnic group to one section and those from another group to a different one. The intention may be to keep people together who are happy working together and may even live in the same communities.

Activity 20

5 mins

In your opinion and experience what are the disadvantages of segregation at work?

_____

_____

_____

You may have highlighted various issues, including the fact that:

■ it could reinforce attitudes about what is suitable or normal work for individuals from particular backgrounds, sex, race or disability;
■ for individuals whose first language is not English, it may prevent improvement of fluency which may limit opportunities for development;
■ it may limit the pool of skills available to the employer by preventing individuals from particular groups ever moving into fields for which they may have an aptitude.

Whatever the reason, segregating employees is illegal and is simply another form of discrimination.

6.7 Review

In this section, you have taken a detailed look at six aspects of illegal discrimination and tested the legal principles against practical situations for all of them. Some of the situations described may be familiar from your own experience, and others may help you anticipate potentially illegal situations which may arise.

The difficulty about many discriminatory practices is that they can be subtle, and may even be justified by those who practise them as a means to achieving harmonious working relationships, for example by keeping people of the same ethnic origins working together.

You need to be on your guard for any form of indirect discrimination to which you may be held to be a party. You can be personally liable in law even when you are not the instigator but are simply obeying a direct order, going along with existing custom and practice or responding to pressure from an individual or a group simply for the sake of making the hard life of a first line manager just that bit easier.

Self-assessment 2 ·

25 mins

1 Fill in the blanks in the following sentence.

The law relating to unfair discrimination sets out to _____ such practices on a number of specified _____ to _____ members of groups whom it defines as having been _____ previously at work.

2 Name four of the eight grounds on which discrimination can be unlawful.

_____

_____

_____

_____

3 In your own words, explain the difference between direct discrimination and indirect discrimination.

_____

_____

_____

4 Complete the following sentences.

Discrimination is justifiable where it is carried out because of the need for a

_____ _____ _____ .

5 The offence of '_____ to discriminate' can only be committed when an order to discriminate is given by someone who is in a position to do so.

6 The Disability Discrimination Act requires employers to make _____ _____ to help disabled employees which treats each _____ on its own _____ .

7 Read each of the following descriptions and then decide whether an offence has been committed. If you think it has, select the correct name for it from the following list.

DISCRIMINATION
INSTRUCTION TO DISCRIMINATE
PRESSURE TO DISCRIMINATE
SEGREGATION
VICTIMIZATION

a One group tries to put pressure on another to discriminate unlawfully, but the unlawful discrimination does not take place.

This is/is not an offence. The correct name for it is

_____

b A group of workers is made up of members from two different countries. There are one or two arguments, so the supervisor separates them and makes them work as separate racial groups.

This is/is not an offence. The correct name for it is

_____

c Someone is accused of unlawful discrimination, but says that he was merely obeying an order from his boss, although he didn't agree with it.

This is/is not an offence. The correct name for it is

_____

d An employee accuses his work mates of unlawful discrimination. They are very angry and respond by 'sending him to Coventry'.

This is/is not an offence. The correct name for it is

_____

8 Name three recent pieces of legislation which could be relevant to illegal discriminatory practices at work

_____

_____

_____

9 Other areas of working life which are being looked at include defining unfair discrimination on the basis of _____, _____ and _____ _____.

10 The Public Interest Disclosure Act, commonly known as the _____ Act, _____ employees who report a wide range of _____ _____ about employment practices.

11 The best way to stay within the law is to manage within both its _____ and _____ and to develop _____ plans to _____ other _____ practices which may break it. It is all part of a modern manager's job.

Answers to these questions can be found on pages 163–4.

7 Summary

- The law defines a number of specific employment practices as illegal and so endeavours to create a level playing field for all people seeking to earn a living through employment.

- **You may be personally liable** if the law on equality is broken in your workplace by you or by someone you supervise.

- The main grounds on which unfavourable discrimination may be unlawful are:

  - sex;
  - marital status;
  - race;
  - colour;
  - nationality;
  - ethnic origin;
  - national origin;
  - disability.

- Discrimination can take any of the following forms:

  - direct discrimination;
  - indirect discrimination;
  - victimization;
  - pressure to discriminate;
  - instruction to discriminate;
  - segregation.

- Commitment by the UK Government to the **European Social Chapter** has entailed various European Directives affecting potential claims of illegal discrimination.

- You should develop **contingency plans** in regard to potential areas of working practices which may be defined as illegal discrimination.

- There can be **no definitive statement** of the law on discrimination since this is in a state of flux and is affected by decisions from employment tribunals and courts, including the European Court of Human Rights.

- As a first line manager you should **manage within the spirit**, as well as the letter, of the law as a demonstration of your commitment to equality at work.

Session C
Pursuing real equality in the workplace

 ## 1 Introduction

Everyone has, at one time or another, been treated in a way which they felt was not fair. It may have been at work or somewhere else. Unfair treatment, whether or not it is sufficiently serious to involve breaking the law, can leave people feeling depressed and angry. The damage that those kinds of feelings can do to people in your work team can be enormous.

So, it's not really safe to assume that just because you are keeping to the laws that protect diversity everyone in your work team must be feeling happy and as if they are a valued part of the team.

Knowing what the law requires of you is one thing. Now we need to look at ways in which you can ensure that you meet your obligations. The same methods will allow you to create a diverse environment in which you and your work team can enact a real commitment to equality.

In this session we will try to answer the following question.

What should a first line manager do to achieve equality in the workplace?

We will need to consider two things.

- Carrying out practices that will ensure there is no unlawful discrimination in the workplace.
- Making the workplace somewhere where everyone really cares about equality, and shows this in their attitudes, behaviour and daily treatment of one another.

2 Who is liable?

As we have already seen, first line managers must always be sure that they do not break the law relating to equality and diversity. They must also avoid helping anyone else to commit an unlawful act, because

anyone who knowingly aids another to commit an unlawful act of discrimination will share liability for that act.

Liability can be **individual** or **vicarious.**

Vicarious liability simply means that whoever is finally responsible for individuals who commit unlawful acts also has responsibility for those acts.

Thus, if employees commit an unlawful act, their employer will also be held responsible.

The following rule applies.

The employer as well as the individual employee is liable for any unlawful act of discrimination committed by the employee unless it is shown that the employer has taken all reasonable practical steps to prevent discrimination occurring.

Let's look at an actual case, now.

EXTENSION 1
Legal liability can involve serious penalties; there is no upper limit to the amount of compensation which can be awarded. There is fuller information about penalties for discriminatory offences in the Extensions section.

Activity 21

5 mins

The following is a case of unlawful discrimination. When you've read it, decide who you think is liable.

> In a workplace, a group of white workers regularly taunted and jeered at an Asian worker, making his life miserable. The team leader never seemed to notice anything, and when eventually the Asian worker complained to him about this treatment the team leader said:
>
> 'You must be imagining it. I know the men – they like a laugh, but that's all there is to it. I've never seen anything going on. You don't want to be too sensitive about these things, you know.'

Eventually the worker left the company, unable to stand the harassment any longer. He then took a case of discrimination to an Industrial Tribunal. During the hearing it was established that:

- there was a high turnover of Asian workers in the work teams in that section, but no information was available as to why they had left;

- the company had no policies or procedures to prevent discrimination occurring; no training or guidance relating to equality at work was given to team leaders; and abusive behaviour of the kind complained of was not a matter of discipline in the company.

The Tribunal found that direct discrimination on grounds of race had occurred.

Who do you think was liable?

The white workers?   YES/NO

The team leader?   YES/NO

The employer?   YES/NO

In this case it was decided that the white workers and the employer shared responsibility.

The **workers** were individually liable because they treated the Asian worker in a less favourable way than they treated other, white workers, without justification.

The **employer** was vicariously liable because the company took no practical steps to make sure that everyone knew and carried out the requirements of the law.

What about the team leader?

You may have been unsure whether the team leader had any liability. In fact the Tribunal might have decided either way. If the Tribunal had decided that the team leader was really unaware what was going on because the white workers were careful not to get caught, he would not have been held liable.

If, on the other hand, he knew what was going on, or had joined in the taunting, he would have been held liable. He could not have claimed ignorance of the law, because ignorance of the law is no defence.

The other important point coming out of this case was that the employer kept no records to show why previous Asian workers had left. Records and up-to-date information should always be available to show exactly what steps have been taken to prevent discrimination in the workplace and to prove how people have been treated at work.

3 Procedures for ensuring equality

In our rule for liability, you will have noted the phrase 'reasonable practical steps'. What this means is that there should be good procedures and practices covering every personnel process in the workplace.

Activity 22 · 4 mins

'Every personnel process' covers a lot of ground. How many aspects of personnel management can you think of that could be relevant to the law on diversity?

I've listed four to get you started. Try to think of **four** more.

- Recruitment
- Selection
- Promotion
- Transfer

_____

_____

_____

_____

The answers to this activity can be found on page 169.

It would be important to have clear procedures and good practices to ensure equality of treatment and opportunity in all of these areas.

But how do we ensure that we are treating everybody equally at all stages? The key word is **objectivity.**

Objectivity means thinking about something without letting your own or anybody else's personal feelings enter into it.

Activity 23

3 mins

During their working lives people are constantly subject to a selection process. They may be selected for: appointment to a job, training, transfer, promotion, redundancy or dismissal.

What do you take into account when **you** select people?

Tick each factor in the list below, according to how relevant you feel it is in your selection process: 'never relevant', 'rarely relevant' or 'possibly relevant'. If you think it is possibly relevant, jot down your reason.

Factors	How relevant is this factor when you are selecting someone			If the factor is possibly relevant
	Never	Rarely	Possibly	Explain why
Has excellent references				
Was recommended by someone you know				
Shares your interests/ outlook/sense of humour				
Has a similar cultural background to the rest of the team				
Colour of skin				
Job record				
Skills in speaking or writing English				
Disciplinary record				

Of course, there can be no right or wrong answers here. It is also probably difficult to be totally honest – we are all influenced by our own prejudices.

However, someone in a position to make decisions about the selection of other people knows how important objectivity is.

If you admitted that you are influenced (for example) by appearance, or skills in English, when these things are not really relevant to the job, then you should be congratulated. At least you have acknowledged your own weakness. Most people try to pretend they are always completely objective.

Relevant factors are the only ones which should be taken into account when making decisions at work.

How can we ensure this happens?

EXTENSION 3
The extension goes into this checklist in much more detail. The checklist itself is based on recommendations from the two Codes of Practice that explain how to avoid discrimination on sex or racial grounds. These Codes of Practice, also discussed in the extension, are well worth looking at because they provide cheap practical guidance on the subject which is regularly updated.

- There should be **procedures** to ensure that there is objectivity and equality of treatment.
- **Training and guidance** should be given in these procedures to everyone who has to carry them out, and to everyone who will be affected by them.
- **Checks** on policy, procedures and practice should take place regularly.
- Corrective **action** must be taken where checks show it to be necessary.
- **Records** must be kept to prove that all reasonable steps have been taken to achieve equality of treatment, and that those steps have been understood and followed.

These principles of good practice can be used as a checklist to make sure there is equality of treatment in personnel processes.

This new five-point checklist is as follows.

1 Identify the **relevant factors**.

2 Install the **procedures**.

3 Provide the **training and guidance**.

4 Carry out regular **checks**.

5 Maintain the **records**.

Activity 24 ·

12 mins

In each of the three cases below, use the five-point checklist to decide the steps to be taken. If you feel that an item on the checklist is relevant to the case, describe briefly the action you would take. If an item on the checklist is **not** relevant to the case, leave it blank.

Case 1

In a factory it was found that Asian job applicants had difficulty in communicating easily in interviews, yet usually turned out to be very good workers.

What should the personnel officer tackle first, in order to make the selection process work better?

■ Identify the relevant **factors**.

_____

_____

■ Install **procedures** to ensure equality and objectivity.

_____

_____

■ Provide **training and guidance** in these procedures.

_____

_____

■ Carry out **checks** to ensure that policies and procedures are working.

_____

_____

■ Make sure that **records** are being maintained.

_____

_____

Case 2

In one company it was found that Kurds who enquired about jobs were usually rejected out of hand by the telephonists, receptionists and even by the gatekeepers. They would say things like: 'The job went yesterday.' or 'Sorry, they're just interviewing for it now.' or 'Don't know which job you mean – there are no vacancies like that here.'

What should be done first to change this situation?

■ Identify the relevant **factors**.

_____

_____

■ Install **procedures** to ensure equality and objectivity.

_____

_____

■ Provide **training and guidance** in these procedures.

_____

_____

■ Carry out **checks** to ensure that policies and procedures are working.

_____

_____

■ Make sure that **records** are being maintained.

_____

_____

Case 3

Asked why so few women, in a large female workforce, became first line managers, one of the managers said: 'Oh, we don't get many applications from them. You know what women are like – they just come here for a bit of extra money and a good natter with their pals. They don't want responsibility.'

But several women, talking the matter over together, said that it was no good applying for promotion because they never got selected. The few who tried were usually told that 'men would react badly to being bossed around by a woman'. They didn't believe it was the true reason though – it was the senior management who were alarmed at the idea of women having any sort of power in the workplace.

What should be done to sort out these problems?

■ Identify the relevant **factors**.

_____

_____

■ Install **procedures** to ensure equality and objectivity.

_____

_____

■ Provide **training and guidance** in these procedures.

_____

_____

■ Carry out **checks** to ensure that policies and procedures are working.

_____

_____

■ Make sure that **records** are being maintained.

_____

_____

Now let us consider the answers to each case.

■ Case 1

The factors relevant to this job certainly need to be identified, because it seems that Asian workers are having trouble with the interviews, yet perform the job well.

Procedures for selection probably need to be changed – perhaps from interviews to tests of some kind.

Once new procedures are installed, training and guidance may need to be given on the best way to use them.

■ Case 2

It looks as though the problems are that either there is no agreed set of procedures or that the agreed procedures aren't being followed by everyone. Procedures should be agreed and no discrimination should be allowed.

Once procedures are established, training and guidance will need to be given in their use.

Checks must then be carried out to ensure that the procedures are being followed.

■ Case 3

The most useful first step will probably be to carry out checks to establish, using a variety of sources, what exactly is going on.

Records will need to be analysed to see how many women apply for posts as first line managers, and what was said at the interviews.

It will also have to be established what factors were used for selection, what procedures for selection have been agreed and whether these procedures have been followed and staff trained in their operation of them.

So, in this last case, all five items on our checklist will need to be used.

Activity 25

**S/NVQ
B11**

This Activity may provide the basis of appropriate evidence for your S/NVQ portfolio. If you are intending to take this course of action, it might be better to write your answers on separate sheets of paper.

Think of an occasion when you have been able to observe a decision-making process to do with selection of an individual for additional training, employment, promotion or for an opportunity to change roles within your work team. Ideally it should be an occasion when you were actively involved in making the decision.

Once you have settled on a specific case, select **two** of the stages on the five-point checklist for ensuring equality of treatment in personnel processes and briefly note how things could have been done differently to ensure equality.

Bear in mind what you have read about 'positive action'. Is this something which could have applied to the case you have chosen to consider?

_____

_____

_____

_____

_____

_____

_____

_____

_____

Your work notes for this activity will provide you with a useful example of points from the checklist being applied to a genuine decision-making process. You could develop it further by repeating the activity using the three items from the checklist which you have not already used. You could then write up the possible improvements which you have identified as a report, clearly presenting your recommendations for improvements and the reasoning behind them.

4 Commitment to equality

Simply making sure that what happens at work is technically within the law isn't really enough to ensure there are good working relationships, nor that the best use is being made of everyone's abilities.

We need commitment to diversity – not only for those whom the law protects, but for all groups and individuals.

Activity 26

The following story illustrates the fact that prejudices may be lurking in the minds of all of us.

> A man was travelling in the Italian Alps in a car with his young son. As he drove along a mountain road, suddenly, without warning, an Alfa Romeo sports car appeared, coming straight at them in the opposite direction. The man swerved to avoid it, and in doing so plunged over the edge of the mountain road. The driver of the Alfa Romeo called an ambulance, but it arrived too late to save the driver, who had died instantly. However, although his eight-year old son was badly injured, with multiple fractures and burns, he was still alive. He was rushed unconscious to the accident department of the nearest hospital, where they decided to operate. As he was wheeled into the theatre, the surgeon who was about to perform the operation saw his face, recognized him and exclaimed: 'My son! My son!'

Who was the surgeon?

People give some very strange answers to this question. Some think that the driver of the car had adopted the boy, or was the wife's second husband. Others say the surgeon had made a mistake – it was just someone who looked like his son. Some have even said that the surgeon was a priest!

In fact, the surgeon was the boy's mother. If you wrote that down, take top marks.

Most people don't get this answer, and it isn't very surprising that they don't. In our society we have ready-made, deeply held ideas about the sort of jobs women hold. We don't think of surgeons as being women.

We tend to have standardized, oversimplified mental pictures of many different groups of people and what they are capable of. These mental pictures are called **stereotypes.**

A typical stereotype of a disabled person, for example, is of someone in a wheelchair, unable to do anything useful and needing help to perform the simplest task. Of course, when we think about it, we realize this is nonsense. We only have to think of some famous 'disabled' people to refute this idea: President Roosevelt, Professor Stephen Hawking, Douglas Bader . . . you may be able to bring to mind many more examples.

Activity 27

10 mins

Managers can often get into difficulties when dealing with applications for employment or promotion from people who do not fit with their stereotype of the kind of person who would normally do that job. This is a problem which is experienced by all of the groups we have discussed in this workbook so far. Let's look at an example.

> A volunteer co-ordinator for a charity providing practical support for people with cancer received an application to work as a volunteer from a man who used a wheelchair. The work involved visiting service users in their homes so mobility, including the ability to drive, was very important. The charity had an equal opportunities policy which the volunteer co-ordinator understood and supported. The volunteer co-ordinator wondered how best to deal with this particular application.

The volunteer co-ordinator had a number of different concerns.

- She didn't want the disabled applicant to be made to feel that his application had created a problem.
- She was reluctant to reject the application simply because of the disability.
- She didn't know how the applicant's disability would actually affect his ability to do all of the things which the work required.
- She didn't feel comfortable with the idea of asking the applicant about his disability and the things which he could and could not do.

How would you have decided to deal with the application?

_____

_____

_____

_____

The real stumbling block which the volunteer co-ordinator came up against was the last point on the list. She didn't feel comfortable with the idea of asking the applicant about his disability and the things which he could and could not do.

Why didn't she feel comfortable discussing the situation? It is not an uncommon reaction but is it a reasonable one?

Lots of people can get embarrassed or nervous dealing with people with disabilities. This can be caused by a fear of saying the wrong thing or by a stereotype which we've already mentioned – if someone is in a wheelchair it is often assumed that they are incapable of communicating or of making decisions.

The other reason for nervousness – being afraid of saying the wrong thing – is also based on assumptions. Realistically, the man is unlikely to be upset by the issue of his disability being raised as long as it is done with an open mind. In fact, he is likely to be very used to discussing his abilities and knows more about his own capabilities than anyone else.

The volunteer co-ordinator in our example interviewed the man in the same way that she would have interviewed anybody else. They discussed the man's particular skills and interests and his suitability for the job in the ordinary way. When the volunteer co-ordinator described what the job actually involved, the man replied by explaining how he could achieve those tasks. Once the capabilities of the applicant were established it didn't take long to make a few arrangements to ensure that potential problems would be avoided. For example, the man was allocated a group of service users to visit whose homes were accessible in a wheelchair.

The interview was actually fairly straightforward once the volunteer co-ordinator realized that this applicant was actually very like any other. It can be very difficult to overcome stereotypes and to remember that any person we meet is **not** necessarily going to fit our assumptions.

If your ideas about how best to deal with the disabled man's application were different from the approach which the volunteer co-ordinator took then you shouldn't worry. There is no perfect answer. However, it is worth looking again at your response and asking whether you were basing your decision on any stereotypes.

The first point in the five-point checklist – identify the relevant factors – was important in this case. Unfortunately the volunteer co-ordinator didn't feel able to identify the relevant factors at first because of her own stereotypical beliefs about a man in a wheelchair.

Activity 28

3 mins

Here are three short cases from quite common work situations. When you've read them, answer the question at the end of each case.

Case 1

Ganesh Patel, a man of Indian origin, started work in a coffee processing plant. The team leader put another worker of Indian origin, Pritpal Singh Dhillon, to work with Patel to show him the job. Patel came to the team leader a couple of days later and said that he would prefer to work with an Englishman because he would show him how to do the job better than Dhillon would. The team leader agreed to this, but was puzzled. He thought, however, that it was typical of Indians that they wouldn't help one another. He supposed Dhillon was reluctant to train Patel in case he worked himself out of a job.

The team leader's analysis of the situation was incorrect. What could have explained Patel's request?

_____

_____

Case 2

A man had worked as an accountant for fifteen years. He was very capable and had a first-class record for time keeping and reliability. Unfortunately the firm he was working for closed. The man applied for another job, but, although he was well qualified to do it, was told by the new company: 'We can't afford to take chances on people like you – we need someone reliable, who isn't going to take a lot of time off.'

Why would a company say such a thing to a job applicant, if he had no record of being unreliable or of taking time off?

_____

_____

Case 3

A woodmill needed to employ another worker. They advertised the post and five experienced lumberjacks were invited to be interviewed. When the final candidate, Pat Wilson, walked into the interview room the interview panel reacted by looking slightly confused. By the time the final question was answered the panel looked entirely uninterested. Pat left feeling sure that the job would go to one of the others.

What might make an interview panel react in this way to an applicant who was as skilled and experienced as the other applicants?

_____

_____

■ Case 1

The truth was that Patel had come to the UK from East Africa in the 1970s when he was quite young, and he spoke excellent English and Gujarati. Dhillon, who had only recently come to the UK from India, spoke Punjabi and his spoken English was not particularly good. So they came from different countries, spoke different languages and had quite different backgrounds. Communication posed problems for them. To the team leader, they were just 'typical Indians', yet they were as different from one another as both were 'different' from the team leader.

■ Case 2

You may have guessed that the man was disabled. The new company's reaction was typical of many – that disabled people are unreliable and take a lot of time off because of sickness. This is rarely true. Disability is not the same thing as sickness. In fact, there are a large number of disabled athletes who are extremely fit.

■ Case 3

The lumberjack who so obviously failed to impress the panel was a woman. The panel's reaction was based on common stereotypes about the kinds of work which are suitable for women.

The cases we have been looking at show how stereotyping at work can lead to harmful attitudes and to discriminatory behaviour.

As a first line manager, you have the chance to take the lead in tackling harmful stereotyping, and the problems of communication and understanding that tend to go with it.

5 Pursuing real equality

EXTENSION 4
Companies and other organizations which have a policy of equal opportunities for all usually set out this policy in a formal statement. An example of such a policy statement is given in the extension.

Stereotyping and discrimination of any kind cannot be got rid of overnight. Generating a real commitment to equality has to be a continuous process.

The first step is to look again at your organization's equal opportunities policy. Having a well thought out equal opportunities policy is very important but it is unlikely to make a real difference to attitudes and practices among your work team unless everyone is aware of it and understands it properly. You have a responsibility to make sure that the policy is not just written down and then forgotten about.

Activity 29   20 mins

Everyone involved in managing others should be familiar with the organization's policy and procedures relating to diversity and equal opportunities in their workplace.

Obtain a copy of your organization's policy and procedures, and make a note of the main points that relate to you and your management role.

_____

_____

_____

_____

_____

_____

You might consider including the main points of the policy and the reasons why it is important in your next team briefing.

Sometimes, it can be very difficult for people who are being treated unfairly to complain about what is happening to them. We have looked at a lot of cases in which one clear example of discrimination has been identified. Here is a slightly different situation.

Sarah Watts worked in the accounts department of a large company. She was the only woman in the department and she shared a large office with five men. The office seemed to most people to have a friendly and jovial atmosphere but Sarah was not happy there. The men with whom she worked enjoyed a joke; the problem was that a lot of the jokes they enjoyed were about women in general and, sometimes, about Sarah in particular. Occasionally, Sarah thought their jokes were quite funny – more often she felt offended. The men also frequently talked about sex in a way which made Sarah feel uncomfortable.

The men were much more familiar with Sarah than they ever were with each other; they often called her 'darling' or 'sweetheart'.

Sarah's manager was also a man. He often joined in with the jokes and he also spoke to Sarah very differently to the way he spoke to the men in the department.

Before long Sarah felt so unhappy at work that she started to look for employment elsewhere.

Most people can 'take a joke' but being the butt of jokes on a regular basis is very different, especially when you are isolated in the way that Sarah was, being the only woman in a group of men.

The conversations about sex which made Sarah feel uncomfortable could easily be seen as sexual harassment. There is no good reason why Sarah should be expected to put up with these things which she did not enjoy – they are not part of the job in an accounts department!

Calling Sarah 'darling' and 'sweetheart' was both patronizing and overly familiar. Affection, in its place, can make people feel wonderful but, in this case, it was clearly misplaced. Terms like 'darling' are not really an appropriate way for people whose relationship is solely professional to address each other. The fact that the men spoke in this way to Sarah but wouldn't address each other with the same degree of familiarity meant that Sarah was being treated differently because of her sex.

Activity 30

5 mins

Sarah discussed the fact that she was not happy at work with a friend who told her that she should make a complaint, either formally or informally.

Sarah considered complaining but felt that it would be too difficult.

Consider Sarah's situation and note some reasons why she might find complaining so difficult.

_____

_____

_____

_____

_____

_____

Sarah was in a very awkward situation. You might have thought of a whole range of reasons why complaining could be difficult. Here are three main reasons.

■ The time never seemed to be right. Sarah was afraid that if she complained after a particular joke or overly familiar remark then she would be told she was over-reacting. This is a major problem with the kind of inequality which was making Sarah so unhappy. A stream of minor incidents can do just as much damage as a major one but can be far harder to address.

■ Sarah felt sure that nobody was deliberately making her unhappy. She was concerned that people at work wouldn't understand why she was making a complaint about behaviour which they obviously thought was perfectly reasonable.

■ Sarah's complaint would have to be addressed, at least in the first instance, to her manager but he was one of the main offenders. Telling a manager that you are unhappy about the behaviour of someone else can be a nerve-wracking process: telling the same person that you're not happy about their behaviour is even harder.

Unfortunately, Sarah's experiences are not as uncommon as you might think and sexual harassment can be a great deal more extreme than Sarah's case. Cases which have been taken to industrial tribunals in the past have detailed years of physical sexual harassment and verbal abuse. First line managers have a responsibility to make sure that a situation like the one we have examined – or worse – does not arise. If action is taken by employees who experience harassment, first line managers who did not attempt to deal with the situation can be considered to share liability.

As a first line manager, you have exactly the same responsibility to all the people in your work team. A crucial point here is **leading by example.**

Whatever you say about equality and fairness will ring hollow if your actions don't match your words. Your work team will take their lead from you, and not practising what you preach could have a serious effect on the way your work team view you. If you seem to be behaving hypocritically then you can't really expect to command the respect of the people who work with you.

Another important reason for considering your own behaviour can be seen in Sarah's case. She was reluctant to approach her first line manager about the problems she had because she was not confident that he would understand and respond in a supportive manner.

Unless people in your work team are confident that you will respond positively to any problems which they might discuss with you, there is a real danger that they will say nothing and that the problems will get worse without you even realizing they exist.

The following reminder list should help you to retain the full confidence of your work team and to play your part in protecting diversity at work:

Explain the main points to everyone in your work team.
Question your own attitudes and assumptions.
Understand the problems facing certain groups at work.
Assess people and situations objectively.
Lead by example.
Influence those in a position to change things.
Treat everyone equally.
You are the key to an improved outlook on equality in your work team.

Activity 31

**S/NVQ
B11**

This Activity may provide the basis of appropriate evidence for your S/NVQ portfolio. If you are intending to take this course of action, it might be better to write your answers on separate sheets of paper.

We have considered a number of ways in which a first line manager can act to ensure that team members are treated fairly and are respected as individuals. Now, think carefully about your own workplace and try to come up with a list of practical steps which you can take. The list should contain as many specific actions as possible.

_____

_____

_____

_____

_____

_____

_____

_____

_____

To develop this activity further you could carry out each of the actions you have listed and keep a record of their effects.

Self-assessment 3 ·

10 mins

Fill in the blanks in the sentences with a suitable word or words.

1 Anyone who knowingly aids another to commit an _____ act of discrimination will share _____ for that act.

2 _____ liability simply means whoever is finally responsible for individuals who commit unlawful acts also has responsibility for those acts.

3 The employer as well as the individual employee is liable for any unlawful act of discrimination committed by the employee unless it is shown that the employer has taken all _____ _____ _____ to prevent discrimination occurring.

4 The five-point checklist is as follows.

   a Identify the **relevant** _____.

   b Install the _____.

   c Provide the _____ and **guidance**.

   d Carry out regular _____.

   e Maintain the _____.

5 Identify the one **false** statement below.

   ■ An employer is not always held responsible when their employee is guilty of unlawful discrimination.

   ■ A first line manager is always responsible for any act of unlawful discrimination by a member of his or her team.

   ■ First line managers are in a position to influence people in taking a less stereotyped view of disadvantaged groups.

Answers to these questions can be found on pages 164–5.

6 Summary

- Anyone who knowingly aids another to commit an unlawful act of discrimination will share liability for that act.

- The employer as well as the individual employee is liable for any unlawful act of discrimination committed by the employee unless it is shown that the employer has taken all reasonable practical steps to prevent discrimination occurring.

- Records and up-to-date information should always be available to show exactly what steps have been taken to prevent discrimination in the workplace and to prove how people have been treated at work.

- The five-point checklist to achieve equality of treatment in personnel processes is as follows.

    1 Identify the **relevant factors**.
    2 Install the **procedures**.
    3 Provide the **training and guidance**.
    4 Carry out regular **checks**.
    5 Maintain the **records**.

Session D
Employment policies

1 Introduction

All organizations must manage their affairs in every respect within the law of the land. In the employment field, there are many statute laws which apply, dealing with matters such as:

■ contracts of employment;
■ terms and conditions of employment;
■ equal opportunities;
■ data protection;
■ dealings with trades unions;
■ health, safety and welfare at work.

The best way for an organization to ensure that it manages within the law is for it to develop employment policies that accord with both the letter and the spirit of existing laws and changes that are known to be forthcoming.

Provided that they do so, and provided that they revise their policies from time to time as the law and regulations change, managers (including you) can be confident that they are managing lawfully by implementing the policies implicitly.

In this session, we'll examine the policies that organizations need to implement, and the records that they need to keep in order to manage within the law.

2 Communicating employment policies

Whether or not an organization writes down its employment policies, it must obey the law consistently and fairly throughout its operations. An important aspect of doing so is communicating those policies to all its employees.

Three effective ways of doing this are through:

- providing an Employee Handbook;
- induction training;
- giving regular briefings to communicate changes in policy.

2.1 The organization handbook

Activity 32

Many references will be made to Employee Handbooks or manuals in this session. Please obtain a copy of your own organization's document to compare this text with. If your organization doesn't have one, then talk to your manager about possible actions once you have completed the session.

Many organizations communicate their employment policies by recording them in a handbook, which is issued to all employees when they first join. This is a crucial aspect of ensuring that everyone gets the same message.

But it isn't sufficient simply to issue an Employee Handbook. That is not considered to be communicating with employees adequately within the law.

Activity 33

3 mins

List three or more factors which may prevent employees from understanding the Employee Handbook issued to them on joining. For example, literacy – not every employee may be able to read, but everyone still needs to understand the organization's policies.

_____

_____

_____

The factors you may have listed include:

- language – some employees may not have English as their first language;
- organizational jargon that is unfamiliar to a newcomer;
- references to the organizational structure and specialist departments, which they are unfamiliar with;
- legalistic phrases such as 'gross misconduct', which may be new to them.

You may well have listed others, thinking back to your own early days with a new employer.

The handbook's content will vary according to the size of the organization and the facilities it is able to provide. But some items should appear in every handbook, especially those concerning health and safety, disciplinary procedures and grievance procedures.

Activity 34 ·

5 mins

What employment procedures do you believe should be covered in an Employee Handbook? Make at least five suggestions.

_____

_____

_____

_____

You may have suggested the following topics: hours of work; reporting absence for sickness or some other reason; holiday entitlement and booking procedure; maternity leave; pension schemes; health and safety; smoking; emergencies; personal hygiene; sports and social facilities; payment procedures; recognized trades unions; disciplinary and grievance procedures; definition of 'gross misconduct'; training and opportunities for development.

A sensible time to issue the Employee Handbook is immediately after induction has taken place.

2.2 Induction training

The importance of induction training as the first step in communicating employment policies cannot be overstated.

Ideally, induction should be delivered before employees begin work, otherwise they may be put at risk through ignorance of safety and emergency procedures. Also, it will be open to individuals to claim that 'nobody told me I wasn't supposed to do that', no matter how obviously wrong their conduct may seem to you.

Though 'ignorance of the *law* is no defence', many employment rules go beyond what the law requires, so ignorance of rules about use of property for personal purposes, or how to report absence, would only put an employee in breach of rules if they had been given reasonable instruction in them.

At induction, the main aspects of the organization's employment policies should be explained by competent managers. The new employees should be given a chance to ask questions and clarify anything which they do not understand. This may be especially important with young employees new to the world of work: they may find it a more disciplined environment than they have been used to.

2.3 Regular briefings

Holding regular meetings with your whole team has many advantages. It encourages team spirit, it makes everyone feel involved, no one has an excuse that they haven't been informed of rules and regulations, and it enables you to obtain feedback about how the team members feel about the organization and the organizational policies that affect them.

3 The contract of employment

EXTENSION 5 and 6
You can get useful information on contracts of employment from the Advisory, Conciliation and Arbitration Service (ACAS).

The contract of employment is a legal document which sets out the agreement between an employer and an employee. In it, the employee agrees to do specified work in return for which the employer provides the necessary facilities to do the job and pays agreed remuneration.

3.1 Written terms and conditions of employment

It is a legal right for all employees working for organizations employing 20 staff or more to be issued with a written statement of terms and conditions of employment. This statement will specify in detail, for the individual employee, the topics covered generally in the Employee Handbook. It should include grievance and disciplinary procedures.

3.2 How can the contract be ended?

The contract can be broken by either party, for example:

- If *employees* fail to return from holiday, and announce that they intend to remain abroad for the next five years, that would effectively break the contract. So would doing work for a competing company, or committing one of the offences defined as 'gross misconduct', such as fighting or deliberately damaging property.
- If the *employer* fails to pay wages as agreed, or requires an employee to do work which training has not been provided for, or which is unsafe or illegal, then the employer will have broken the contract.

The simplest way for the contract to be ended is for the employee to resign, giving the notice required under the contract.

3.3 What remedies are available for breaches of contract?

If an employee breaks the contract, the remedies available to the *employer* will depend on the disciplinary procedures agreed. If the breach is sufficiently serious, dismissal is always available as the final sanction.

For the *employee*, there may be a remedy through the agreed grievance procedure. If the employee has been dismissed, or has resigned because they believe it is impossible to continue working for the employer, they can apply to an Employment Tribunal (formerly known as an Industrial Tribunal) for a remedy for unfair dismissal. The Tribunal may make an award in the employee's favour if they can convince its members that their case is a just one.

4 Employment Tribunals

Employment Tribunals are legal bodies appointed to adjudicate on legal disputes involving unfair dismissal, victimization, and discrimination on grounds of race, sex or disability. They consist of a 'chair', who is legally qualified, sitting with two other people: one with commercial experience and the other with a practical trade union background.

5 Grievance and disciplinary procedures

This session gives you a brief introduction to formal grievance and disciplinary procedures. You will learn more about them, and about the informal steps you can take in a disciplinary situation, in the rest of this workbook.

5.1 Formal grievance procedures

Formal grievance procedures are an important part of good practice within an organization's employment policies. They offer employees who feel that they are being unfairly treated the chance to raise the matter with their own management.

A credible grievance procedure has a number of stages, allowing the employee to raise their concern:

■ initially with their immediate supervisor, team leader or manager;
■ if that does not resolve the problem, then with the next manager in the hierarchy;
■ and ultimately with a designated senior manager, possibly in the Personnel or Human Resources department.

Informal grievance procedures are a very important aspect of positive employment relations and, as such, will be dealt with more fully in Session B. Fairly implemented, they can prevent minor issues from growing into major ones that may become subject to the formal disciplinary procedure.

5.2 Formal disciplinary procedures

A common misconception is that discipline is about 'punishing' an individual for doing wrong. In fact, the aim of an effective disciplinary procedure is to help employees return to acceptable standards in whatever area necessary.

EXTENSION 7
ACAS is an independent body that can conciliate in employment matters. It produces a number of booklets to help managers work effectively within the law.

The Advisory, Conciliation and Arbitration Service (ACAS) publishes a Code of Practice on disciplinary procedures. Employers who follow this Code, both to the letter and in spirit, are likely to achieve more harmonious relationships with their employees and be able to show that they are managing within the law.

It is vital that you understand your organization's grievance and disciplinary procedures, as they may well affect you directly in your day-to-day activities.

5.3 Stages in the disciplinary procedure

The ACAS Code describes four stages in the disciplinary procedure.

1 For a minor offence, a **verbal warning** or admonishment should suffice. In practice, it is prudent to record that such a warning has been issued.

2   For repeated minor offences, or a single more serious offence, a **first written warning** may be issued, setting a timetable for improvement (indicating any help which may be given to the individual by way of training or support).

3   For repeated offences, or a serious first offence just falling short of dismissal, a **final written warning** may be given, again setting a timetable for improvement and stating that further offences of this kind or related offences may result in dismissal or other penalty such as suspension without pay (if allowed for in the contract of employment).

4   **Dismissal** is the final stage, when all previous stages have been exhausted and further offences have been committed within any final improvement period that has been set.

Summary dismissal, which is dismissal without notice, may be used only in a case of bad conduct that is so serious (gross misconduct) that it requires the employee to be removed immediately from the organization.

Activity 35

Who in your organization has the authority to *dismiss* an employee and what authority do *you* have to impose disciplinary sanctions (for example, a recorded verbal warning or first written warning)?

_____

_____

_____

Your answer will vary according to the policies and procedures of your own organization.

Normally, the authority of a team leader or first line manager will be limited to issuing a verbal warning or admonition. This provides a check on employers, because it protects employees from being sacked or disciplined severely by an immediate superior who may bear a personal grudge against them. The same principle applies at every level. For example, a first line manager should not normally be dismissed by the manager to whom he or she reports without reference to a higher level of management.

5.4 Appeals procedure

To be perceived as fair within the law, an employee should have a right to appeal within a specified period (normally two days) to a senior manager.

This provides a further check on managers by offering employees an opportunity to seek an independent review of a decision that may affect their future career with the company. Employment Tribunals will take the existence of an appeals procedure into account when considering cases of unfair dismissal.

5.5 Applying disciplinary policies and procedures fairly and consistently

Employment Tribunals look to see that procedures, however reasonable they may be in *theory*, are applied fairly and consistently in *practice*. If they are not, then they will not be accepted as meeting the requirements of the law.

Activity 36

5 mins

An organization recently dismissed a long serving employee, Sarah Cole, for persistent lateness, after a final written warning had not brought about any improvement. She applied to an Employment Tribunal, claiming unfair dismissal, bringing two employees as witnesses, both of whom had two final written warnings on file but had not been dismissed.

How do you think the Tribunal would have found, and why?

_____

_____

_____

Almost certainly, the Tribunal would have found in Sarah's favour. This is because the procedures, though reasonable in themselves, had not been applied consistently. Sarah had been dismissed but her two colleagues had not, even though they had also received two written warnings. The records proved that the organization had not applied its own rules consistently.

6 Dealing with recognized trades unions

Under defined conditions, a trade union may apply to the Central Arbitration Committee for legal recognition. Many employers grant recognition voluntarily. In a dispute ACAS can help the parties to reach a mutually acceptable agreement.

Where a trade union has legal recognition, or has been granted representation rights by your organization, it will have the right to take up grievance and disciplinary matters on behalf of its members, initially through the local shop steward.

If you work within a unionized workplace, or are a member of a union yourself, you will know that unions can help to provide an orderly working environment. Shop stewards, safety representatives and union officials are usually well trained in the organization's policies and procedures and the laws that underpin them. They can help you in your efforts to manage employees fairly and consistently.

6.1 Members of trades unions without legal recognition or representation rights

You may work with people who are members of a trade union that is not recognized by your employer and that does not have representation rights for employees who belong to it.

They may belong to an unrecognized union because of the benefits it offers, or they may have stayed in a union which was recognized by a former employer.

A union that is not 'recognized', in the legal sense, does not have a legal right to take up issues on behalf of the employee. This is true even if a number of employees belong to it, unless it has been granted representation rights specifically to act in individual cases of grievance or discipline.

You need to be sure what situation members of your team are in concerning trade union rights.

7 Employment records

A prudent employer will keep accurate and up-to-date records of individual employees, starting from the very beginning of employment.

The records should always include an acknowledgement from the employees that they have received a copy of the Employee Handbook and have had its contents explained to them.

For any disciplinary process to withstand scrutiny by an Employment Tribunal, there must be accurate records of disciplinary actions involving every individual.

Activity 37

5 mins

State, in your own words, why it is important for an employer to keep up-to-date written records of each employee's progress and conduct throughout his or her period of employment. Draw on your own experience, wherever possible, as an employee and a manager.

_____

_____

_____

You may have included issues such as the following: memories are imperfect over a period of time; employees may deny being told something (such as a disciplinary warning) if there is no written proof; an employer may claim that an employee was told something which they deny.

In practice, for most people, there will be nothing to record in a well run organization; but for those employees who cannot, or will not, comply with the organization's rules, there must be a written record of actions taken.

Similarly, there must be a record available of any grievances raised by an employee and of the action taken to try to resolve it.

The records need to comply with the requirements of the Data Protection Act.

7.1 Exit interviews

It is good practice, with their consent, to conduct an exit interview with all employees who leave of their own volition. Exit interviews can provide valuable information about the attitudes of employees since they now have nothing to lose by being frank. A record of the interview can also be valuable if they change their minds later on as to why they left the organization. This is particularly important if they go on to pursue a claim to an Employment Tribunal for unfair dismissal.

Self-assessment 4

20 mins

1   Fill in the three blanks in the following sentence.

The law impinges on many aspects of employing people, including:

a _____

b _____

c _____

2   Suggest three ways in which an employer can ensure that its employment policies are communicated effectively to all employees.

_____

_____

_____

3 _____, _____, and
_____ are three of the main grounds on which
an employee can make an application to an Employment Tribunal.

4 How can well-established grievance procedures help an organization manage
legally?

_____

_____

5 The main stages in a formal disciplinary procedure as recommended by ACAS
are:

1 _____

2 _____

3 _____

4 _____

6 A major principle of sound disciplinary procedures is that _____
is allowed to dismiss their _____ subordinate without reference
to a higher level of management.

7 No matter how good a disciplinary procedure is, it will not be effective legally
unless it is applied _____ and _____.

8 Written records of disciplinary procedures used in relation to an individual
employee are essential to prove to an _____ that an organization
has acted fairly.

9 Appeal procedures are an essential part of _____ procedures if
they are to be seen as fair by an _____.

10 Membership of an employment tribunal comprises a _____ who
is legally qualified; a second member with _____ and a third who
has a _____ background.

Answers to questions can be found on pages 165–6.

8 Summary

- For an organization to comply with the letter and spirit of the many laws touching on employing people, it is essential that it has:

  - policies and procedures founded on best practices such as ACAS codes of practice;
  - means of communicating them intelligibly to all employees, such as an Employee Handbook;
  - induction training;
  - employee briefing systems to keep everyone up to date with changes which will affect them;
  - records of all actions taken under disciplinary procedures;
  - evidence that it applies its policies fairly and consistently.

- The four stages in the formal disciplinary procedure are:

  1 verbal warning;
  2 first written warning;
  3 second written warning;
  4 dismissal.

Session E
The consequences of illegal discrimination

1 Introduction

The financial and other consequences for organizations and individuals resulting from illegal discrimination can be dire, as this real-life case study illustrates.

> In 1997, a company director was found guilty by an employment tribunal of sexual harassment against a female employee. She had resigned and claimed constructive dismissal. The tribunal awarded more than £30,000 in compensation to the victim.
>
> In an attempt to avoid paying her, the director wound up his company, re-established it in another limited company guise and resumed trading.
>
> In 2001, he was found guilty of fraudulent trading and jailed for seven months. He was forced to pay the compensation, plus additional legal charges of around £3,000 to the victim's solicitors. Had he not done so, the judge warned him that he would be jailed for 20 months.

This case shows that, however ingenious or devious you may be, the law can find ways of pursuing you to an ultimate conviction. And remember that, if the offender had not behaved so crassly in the first place, the events which landed him eventually in jail would never have been set in train.

Constructive dismissal occurs when an employer does something which effectively makes it impossible for an employee to carry on working for them, for example relocating a disabled employee to a remote location without a car.

In 2002, the maximum award which can be made by an employment tribunal for unfair dismissal is £50,000. This figure is subject to review, and does not include legal or other costs.

1.1 Remedies for unfair dismissal

Unfair dismissal

In cases where an Employment Tribunal finds that an employee has been unfairly dismissed or forced to resign, it has three remedies at its disposal:

- financial compensation;
- reinstatement;
- re-engagement.

Financial compensation

The tribunal has powers to make an financial award which has a substantial upper limit and to which can be added legal costs and many other expenses.

If the Tribunal finds that disability, race or sex discrimination was involved, then the award made has no upper limit. It can amount to hundreds of thousands of pounds and, in exceptional cases, has exceeded £1 million.

Reinstatement

'Reinstatement' means that employees must be taken back into the job they had at the time of dismissal as though they had never been away from it. They would therefore receive their existing benefits in terms of salary, holiday accruals, pension contributions and all other benefits of service. This would apply even if the employees had been dismissed or had resigned many months previously. If the employer refused to take them back, the Tribunal would increase the alternative award of compensation.

> In 2002, a female bank employee was awarded more than £1 million against her former employer for unfair dismissal involving sex discrimination.

> An Asian policeman received an out of court settlement of more than £200,000 and a personal apology from his chief constable to his entire family. The policeman had been wrongly accused of sending racist hate mail.

Activity 38 · 5 mins

Describe in your own words what the consequences of being ordered to reinstate an employee might be in your own team.

- For you.
- For the team members.
- For your employer.

Think hard about it – the implications are considerable.

_____

_____

_____

_____

You may have said that, for you, there would be 'loss of face', humiliation and possible disciplinary action if you are adjudged by your employer to have been at fault.

For the members of your team the consequences could be possible resentment between them and the reinstated member, re-adjustment to his or her presence, and loss of co-operation with you if they believe that you were in the wrong.

Your employer would have to deal with problems about what to do with any member of staff who had been appointed to replace the reinstated member. The employer would also have to cover the costs of making up lost earnings for the reinstated member, and deal with humiliation and loss of respect from the employees generally. It might even be necessary to make the replacement employee redundant.

The implications are widespread and not all directly quantifiable. For example, loss of respect from a work team can have profound effects on the manager involved. And public humiliation is no laughing matter. Just imagine the feelings of senior managers if they were obliged to make personal apologies to junior employees.

One thing you weren't asked to assess was the effect on those people who are reinstated. For them, it can be an uncomfortable and humiliating experience, and this is why many former employees don't seek or welcome it as a remedy.

Re-employment

Under this remedy, the Tribunal orders the employer to take back the employee, but not necessarily into the same job on the same conditions and benefits of service. It could be into a lower paid job, or one which did not offer benefits such as a company vehicle.

Activity 39

3 mins

At present, a Tribunal cannot **compel** an employer to reinstate or re-employ a former employee, but it is under consideration for the future.

Why do you think an employment tribunal would offer the lesser penalty of re-employment rather than reinstatement?

_____

_____

There could be many reasons, but they will probably all have in common the fact that the employee had contributed in some measure to his or her own downfall, for instance by having a poor disciplinary record or having contributed in some way to the incident leading to dismissal.

Alternatively (or additionally), it may be that the employee deserved the extreme penalty of dismissal, but your organization didn't have adequate procedures or records, hadn't implemented its procedures or couldn't prove that it had done so.

The re-employment of a former employee can cause as much embarrassment as reinstatement, including problems with re-allocating work and soured working relationships. The employer must also bear the tangible costs, which will have already been borne, of legal fees and costs of attending tribunal hearings.

1.2 Consequences of unfair discrimination

A senior barrister was found guilty in 2002 of race discrimination by the Bar Council and suspended from practising for a year because he had called a solicitor's clerk a 'blackamoor' during an Old Bailey trial. He was fined £1,000 – to which must be added **substantial** loss of earnings.

In this short introduction, you have seen that there can be severe consequences for:

- employers;
- senior staff;
- first line management;

for failing to comply with legislation intended to protect employees from unfair discrimination at work.

These consequences can include:

- financial penalties which, in some cases, could affect the viability of the whole business;
- organizational problems, which divert the time of senior managers who should be doing more constructive things;
- loss of respect and, for first line managers, loss of confidence – especially for those who were in any way associated with the breach of the law.

2 Types of liability for illegal discrimination

In law, an organization can be held liable for illegal discrimination in a number of ways.

2.1 Direct liability

An aggrieved employee can bring an action directly against the former employer by making an application to an Employment Tribunal.

2.2 Vicarious liability

If the employer is a limited company, the discrimination can only have been carried out by a human being at some level, or levels, in its organization. The law states that an organization is liable for the actions of its managers and employees at all levels. If it fails to prevent them from committing the unlawful act of discrimination it cannot claim, say, through a senior manager, that it was 'unaware' of the practice complained of.

This legal principle, of an organization being responsible for the wrongful acts of its employees, is known as 'vicarious liability'.

A moment's reflection will convince you that the law cannot allow an employer to claim it did not know what was going on, save in the most exceptional of circumstances. Otherwise no employer could effectively be held responsible for anything that happens at work.

Consider a situation where an accident has happened. A machine has been used in an unsafe condition, with safety systems overridden and guards out of place, leading to a serious injury. It would be very convenient for the management to claim that they did not know what was happening. But, in law, they cannot do so because the organization is vicariously liable for the actions of its employees.

2.3 Personal liability

This was touched on in Session B and is well worth repeating. Any individual can have personal liability for instigating, or colluding with, an act of illegal discrimination.

This can happen if that person:

- issues an instruction to discriminate;
- accepts an order to discriminate;
- bows to pressure from another individual or a group to discriminate illegally;
- takes discriminatory action on his or her own behalf.

Look at the following case study, which is based very closely on a real incident that appeared before an Employment Tribunal.

Activity 40 · 5 mins

A female employee claimed that sex discrimination was the reason she was selected for redundancy ahead of six male employees with similar service and experience. She had been the only woman in a department of more than 200 employees. She said she had to eat her lunch in the ladies' room because the men watched hard core pornographic videos during their meal breaks. She found the videos offensive and degrading.

Her first line manager allegedly told her 'No one wants you here because you're a girl'. Another manager told her that he was embarrassed about the videos, but 'did not want to upset the lads'. He told the tribunal that it upset the men to be forced to turn the video off on her account. The employer claimed to be unaware of the videos and said that she was made redundant because the men who were considered for redundancy were better qualified to do the job.

1   In whose favour do you think the Tribunal would find?

2   Who within the organization might be held liable?

3   Do you believe the Tribunal would order reinstatement, re-employment or make a financial award to the applicant?

1   _____

2   _____

3   _____

This case highlights the issues discussed so far in a remarkably clear manner. The outcome from a Tribunal is never certain but, assuming that the people quoted were telling the truth (and all of them were speaking on oath, of course) the probable outcomes would be as follows.

1   The Tribunal would find in favour of the female applicant.

2   The employer would be held vicariously liable for the actions of its employees because:

■ the senior management should never have allowed such video screenings to become entrenched 'custom and practice';

■ the selection for redundancy would almost certainly prove to be illegal discrimination and tantamount to an instruction to discriminate;

■ the first line manager would be personally liable for bowing to pressure to discriminate;

■ the team members would be personally liable for applying the pressure to discriminate.

3 Reinstatement would probably be an appropriate remedy but it is questionable whether the employee would want to return to such a hostile environment. A substantial award would probably be made instead.

Another factor which the tribunal might have considered is the fact that the employee was the only female in a department of 200 people. As such, the management might have been expected to take some reasonable positive step to ensure that she did not suffer disadvantage.

3 The financial consequences

Recently an award of more than £79,000 was made to an employee of a local authority for disability discrimination. The council had not made 'reasonable adjustment' to accommodate a wheelchair. The award included a sum for hurt feelings.

Financial awards made by tribunals reflect at least in part the earnings potential of the employee. The very large awards sometimes made are usually to employees with high salaries, bonus earnings and other benefits which they have lost by losing the job. However, the Tribunal can also take into account more subjective matters such as hurt feelings, which are not related to earnings ability. For example, an award of around £200,000 made to a headmaster for unfair dismissal included £18,000 for hurt feelings.

Though very large awards are rare, an organization which transgresses the discrimination legislation frequently could find itself paying a number of substantial awards over a period of time. They could soon reach a total to compare with the ones that make the national headlines, and which hurt the organization's profits as severely.

3.1 Ability to pay

Tribunals are under no obligation to consider the ability of an organization to pay, whether it is large or small. Nor will they take into account the nature of the employer's activities. So a charity which employs people must obey the law just as much as school or other employer in the public sector.

The consequences for a non-profit making organization are as serious as for a commercial company. Just think how many books, or how much extra

You are recommended to read the local and national press which publish accounts of Employment Tribunal hearings. They will keep you up-to-date with the way case law is developing and some pitfalls to watch out for in your own workplace.

curricular activity, the £200,000 lost by the school in the example above would have paid for. The headmaster had been replaced, so it didn't save his salary.

To illustrate how costly an award can be, take the following example.

> A tribunal has ordered a retail company to pay compensation to a former employee of £18,000 plus £2,000 in legal fees and other costs. If its normal profit margin is £1 on every £20 taken through the till, it must sell £400,000 extra simply to recover the cost of the awards.

This may be even harder for the company than it looks. Any bad publicity attending the hearings may put customers off. Employment Tribunal hearings are always big news locally, especially where discrimination cases are concerned.

3.2 Implications of illegal discrimination

This section has shown just how dire the financial consequences of breaking the laws on illegal discrimination can be. The risks are not theoretical. They are very real and they are realized for a large number of organizations every year. Although some frivolous and worthless cases are pursued, many of the ones that reach employment tribunals are successful because they are based on the clear legal principles described in this workbook.

The financial problems caused by a relatively modest award can be serious and in some cases life threatening for an entire site or business. Failing to manage to the letter and within the spirit of the law on illegal discrimination has legal, ethical and commercial implications for every manager.

4 The legal process – Employment Tribunals

To most people the most familiar aspect of the legal process will be the Employment Tribunal. Appearance before a tribunal is one of the severest consequences of alleged illegal discrimination. Sometimes individuals who feel aggrieved will argue their own case, but frequently they will employ a solicitor or obtain help from the Citizens' Advice Bureau or their trade union.

The Equal Opportunities Commission and the two other Commissions set up to deal with discrimination matters in regard to race or disability may also provide support where they believe that wider issues of policy or public interest may be involved.

If both you and your organization manage according to the principles and advice given in this workbook, there is a much smaller chance that you will ever encounter a Tribunal in practice, but it is as well to be aware of what could happen.

4.1 The make-up of employment tribunals

A Tribunal comprises a legally qualified 'chair' sitting with two colleagues, one of whom usually has a business or commercial background and one who has practical experience within a trade union. Their combination of skills and experience makes them well qualified to judge the issues and see through any irrelevant arguments advanced by the two parties.

4.2 Who can apply to a tribunal?

In the year 2000/2001 there were more than 17,500 complaints of illegal discrimination, 20% up on the previous year. Half concerned sex discrimination.

In practice, most employees and potential employees can apply to a tribunal, either directly or with the support of the Equal Opportunities Commission (EOC), the Commission for Racial Equality (CRE), the Disabilities commission (DDC) or the Citizens' Advice Bureau.

In general, there is a service qualification period of 12 months for many cases and a maximum period of time (three months) within which to file an application after the alleged offence has occurred.

In practice, both of these requirements are frequently ignored by Tribunals and it is very hazardous for an employer to rely on either.

Under the anti-discrimination legislation, applicants are not subject to any qualification period, as they are performing a 'protected act' within the law. So it is best for you to assume that anyone who believes that they have suffered illegal discrimination on any of the grounds discussed above has a right to appeal to an Employment Tribunal.

4.3 What the tribunal will look for in discrimination cases

The tribunal members follow a strictly logical process to test whether direct or indirect illegal discrimination has taken place. They will compare the applicant with a hypothetical 'comparator'.

Direct discrimination

The Tribunal members will ask themselves, in essence, the following questions.

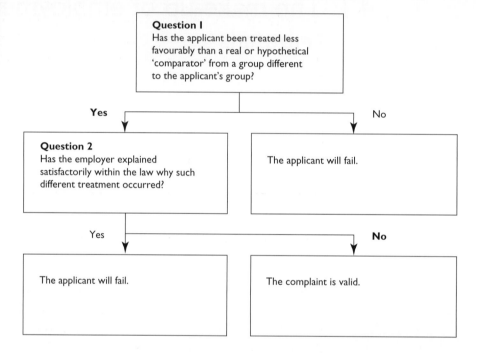

If the answer to question 1 is Yes, and the answer to question 2 is No, then the complaint will succeed and the financial consequences discussed earlier will follow.

Now try applying those two questions above to this short case study.

> An applicant to a Tribunal claimed that he was discriminated against because of his race during a competitive panel interview for an internal promotion. He claimed that the panel allowed him less time than the other four candidates, all of whom were white. In addition, the panel spoke very rapidly and asked him questions which were irrelevant to the post – largely about his interests and affiliations outside work, including his political views. In disgust, he resigned and eventually claimed constructive dismissal through racial discrimination.

His employers broadly accepted the facts of the case but claimed that he had less to say than the other applicants and so the interviewers had filled in time to spare him embarrassment. They also said that he did not match the requirements of the post (though his experience and qualifications were admittedly similar), and that was why he was turned down. They claimed to be an equal opportunities employer.

Activity 41

3 mins

1   On the balance of probabilities, was the applicant treated less favourably than a real or hypothetical 'comparator' from a group different to that of the applicant? (In this case there is a real comparator, i.e. any of the four other applicants.)

2   If Yes, did the employer explain satisfactorily within the law why such different treatment occurred?

The answer to question 1 is most probably Yes, according to the evidence admitted by the employer.

As far as question 2 is concerned, the employer's explanation appears thin. The panel had asked irrelevant questions which could have no bearing on the job and they admitted that his qualifications and experience were similar to the white applicants. Why then should he have had less to say or been given less time to answer relevant questions?

On the balance of probabilities, the answer to question 2 is No, the employer has not given a satisfactory answer within the law.

So in this case, the Tribunal would probably find for the applicant on the basis of **direct racial discrimination.**

Indirect discrimination

Cases of indirect discrimination are often more complicated, as the claimed discrimination is masked by conditions which may or may not be essential to the job. Tribunal members will ask themselves, in essence, the following questions.

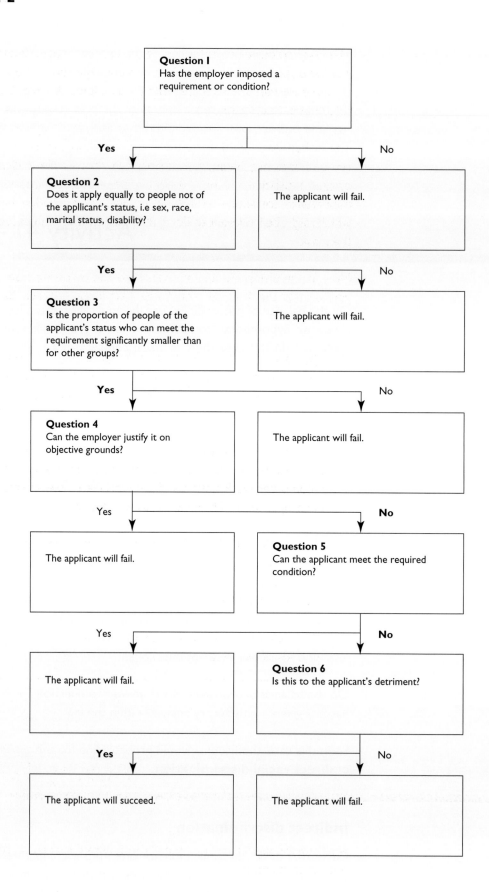

The diagram on page 92 shows that the process is much more complex than it is for direct discrimination. If the tribunal's questioning leads it through the series of answers shown in the diagram then it will find that illegal indirect discrimination has occurred.

The Tribunal's inquisition has to be more thorough because requirements or conditions may be imposed deliberately to mask illegal discrimination. The original legislation did not recognize indirect discrimination, which left the opportunity for those so inclined to hide discrimination behind conditions which might be irrelevant to doing the job. It is the Tribunal's job to look behind the mask.

Now, try applying the logical process to the following case study and say if you believe the Tribunal would find that illegal indirect discrimination had occurred.

> The applicant had applied for an internal vacancy. The job specification stated that the applicant must be 'energetic' and 'able to withstand physically demanding conditions while conducting workplace risk assessments' on a multi-level animal feed mill.
>
> The applicant, who suffered from birth defects caused by thalidomide, believed that neither was necessary. Most of the analysis was done at a computer work station and the workplace assessments were done in co-operation with the local working teams.
>
> She was turned down for the job and resigned shortly afterwards, claiming constructive dismissal. Her employers did not dispute the broad facts but said that, regrettably, they did not believe she could cope with the physical rigours of the job.
>
> The applicant claimed that she had been discriminated against on the grounds of her disability.

Activity 42

5 mins

Applying the logical process, would the applicant succeed in her claim for indirect discrimination?

Applying the logical process, to this case, the answers seem to be as follows.

1 Had the employer imposed a requirement or condition? Yes. In fact, they imposed two conditions, and they did not dispute this.

2 Did it apply equally to people not of the applicant's status? Yes. The conditions applied universally, so no question of direct discrimination arose.

3 Was the proportion of people of the applicant's status who could meet the requirement significantly smaller than for other groups? Yes. The proportion of disabled people able to comply would be much lower.

4 Could the employer justify it on objective grounds? No. It depends whose version you believe – a detailed analysis of the job would be required, but it seems probable here that the physical rigours of the job had been over-stated. The employer might have been able to make 'reasonable adjustments'.

5 Could the applicant meet the requirement or condition? No. It is not disputed that the applicant could not do so.

6 Was this to the applicant's detriment? Yes. It was, as it effectively precluded her from obtaining the post.

Again, taking the balance of probabilities, the employer did not give a satisfactory answer within the law, and in this case the Tribunal would find for the applicant on the basis of **indirect disability discrimination.**

4.4 Victimization

The word 'victimization' has a specific meaning in the laws dealing with illegal discrimination. It occurs where employees take a particular action (known as a 'protected act') in the course of asserting their rights under the Sex Discrimination Act, Race Relations Act or Equal Pay Act, or if they give information to any of the Commissions (EOC; CRE; DDC).

For example, a former employee was awarded £195,000 for victimization when her former employer refused to give her a reference. She had previously committed a protected act by complaining successfully of sex discrimination against her.

It is illegal for an employer to 'victimize' any employee who performs a protected act, and dismissal for doing so would be automatically unfair.

Another automatically unfair reason for dismissal is pregnancy or taking maternity leave.

The test which an Employment Tribunal must apply is straightforward. If the Tribunal's questioning leads it through the series of Yes answers, then the Tribunal must find for the applicant, and the employer must be guilty of victimization within the special meaning assigned by law.

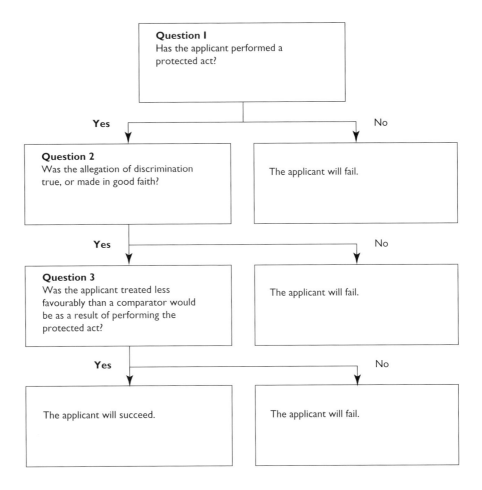

Remember, victimization has a special meaning in law, it is not about being 'picked on' or harassed in the general sense. Applicants merely have to act in good faith – they can even make an allegation which is wildly inaccurate, so long as they believe it to be true.

For someone who has been victimized, it is likely that a Tribunal will order reinstatement as being an appropriate remedy. The protections offered are similar to those under the Public Interest Disclosure Act (PIDA) discussed in Session B, which could be used similarly to report perceived abuses in more general ways, possibly affecting other individuals or groups.

4.5 'On the balance of probabilities'

This phrase has been used a number of times in this section. It is the test used by Tribunal members when deciding whether or not discrimination has taken place. It is not just the facts of a specific incident that are taken into account, but background information about the employee's disciplinary record and circumstantial evidence bearing on the case.

In one year, more than 130,000 cases were taken to employment tribunals. That's 2,500 per week or 500 employers (and their staff) per working day who found themselves facing a Tribunal.

The overall question which the Tribunal must decide is as follows.

'Has the employer acted reasonably on the balance of probabilities which can be inferred from the evidence presented?'

If the answer is 'yes', then the Tribunal will find in favour of the employer; if 'no', then it will find in favour of the applicant.

'On the balance of probabilities' represents a lower standard of proof than that required in a criminal court. It means that a manager can dismiss an employee if he or she genuinely believes that it is 'most probable' that the employee committed an offence. There is no requirement to prove guilt beyond reasonable doubt because if this were applied to employee relations it would be extremely difficult to operate most existing disciplinary procedures.

4.6 Review of Employment Tribunals

There is no real escape from the hard logic of the tests which Employment Tribunals will apply to claims regarding illegal discrimination. They must work in this clear, analytical way to determine, to the best of their abilities, complex cases which could, on the one hand, see a 'failed' applicant's employment prospects potentially in ruins and, on the other hand, impose potentially crippling financial burdens on an employer, regardless of its ability to bear them.

Though there is an appeal process to the Employment Appeal Tribunal (EAT) it is seldom used, so the Tribunal is for practical purposes the end of the legal line.

We have looked in detail at Tribunal procedures because appearance before them is one of the most serious consequences for any organization which fails to comply with the law regarding illegal discrimination.

5 Employment practices and procedures

By now, you should have a detailed picture of the consequences for organizations and individuals of transgressions of the discrimination legislation. This section will look at some ways by which you can help ensure that they are unlikely to affect your organization or yourself.

There are a number of areas to which you should pay close attention.

5.1 Recruitment

The facts of tribunal settlements suggest that awards are increased where an employer has ignored complaints of discrimination in the first instance. First line managers are often the first managers to hear of grievances and their response can be crucial.

Some practices are almost inevitably discriminatory and are mentioned by the Commissions as ones to avoid. 'Word of mouth' advertising about a job, 'father to son' practices or recruitment solely from among members of a particular union can limit the pool of potential applicants to a particular group and discriminate against others.

It is far better practice to advertise all jobs openly, taking care not to use language or state conditions implying that the job is not effectively open to members of some groups.

5.2 Custom and practice

Long established custom and practice can lead to stereotyping of the kind of employee who can do a job. It can take many potentially discriminatory forms such as the following examples.

- 'Women aren't strong enough to drive our heavy goods vehicles'.
- 'Men are never employed as secretaries or personal assistants here'.
- 'Disabled people can't work on our shop floor'.
- 'Our customers won't talk to anyone who isn't the same as they are'.
- 'Only women ever work as receptionists here'.
- 'We've never had a senior manager here who was female'.
- 'We always help women over flexible working hours here – men don't need that sort of concession'.

Activity 43

3 mins

Try to think of any examples of 'custom and practice' from your own experience which could lead, intentionally or not, to illegal discrimination on the grounds of:

1   sex;

2   marital status;

3   equal pay;

4   race;

5   disability.

1 _____

2 _____

3 _____

4 _____

5 _____

Obviously there can be no definitive answer to this activity. It is intended to make you think hard about your own situation and anticipate consequences which might arise from long established practices and attitudes. If you are concerned about any of them, you should take action (directly where possible) and talk to your manager if you need further help.

5.3 Harassment and bullying

EXTENSION 8
ACAS publishes a useful guide on bullying and harassment for managers and employees.

First line managers are particularly well placed to see the signs of potential problems and use their experience and judgement to take appropriate action before the problem actually arises. They must lead by example and neither initiate nor condone practices which could lead to claims of bullying or harassment, whether physical or psychological.

Harassment and bullying can take a variety of forms, and individuals can respond to them quite differently. Nevertheless, you need to be aware of what is happening and sensitive to the reactions which they may cause. Examples could include the following.

A senior manager claimed that he sent pornographic emails 'only to staff who he knew liked them'. A female employee who said she received 100 of them a week and objected strongly to them claimed they amounted to sexual harassment in her claim of unfair dismissal and illegal sex discrimination.

- Initiation rites at the end of training or apprenticeship schemes.
- Telling offensive jokes with sexual, religious, racial or disability connotations.
- Circulating pornographic materials, magazines etc., or showing pornographic videos.
- Making unwelcome, persistent advances to members of the opposite – or same – sex during working hours or at social functions connected to work.
- Physical intimidation to get better paid work, or to obtain 'commission' for obtaining employment from a new recruit.
- Using offensive nicknames based on race, sex or physical characteristics.
- Persistent foul language and crude behaviour.

All these behaviours can, and in many cases have, led to the doors of the Employment Tribunal and had serious consequences for employers and managers. Many of them go far beyond what it is reasonable to expect any employee to regard as a 'joke', and managers at all levels have been implicated in offensive or aggressive behaviour. Many of the behaviours could even represent gross misconduct which merits summary dismissal.

5.4 Appraisal systems

Used positively, appraisal processes should be a force for promoting equality of opportunity. However, if the interview is not handled with sensitivity, or a feeling develops that members of one group seem never to receive favourable assessments or gain promotion, then the system itself (or those implementing it) may come to be suspected of using it to disadvantage particular groups.

5.5 Stress at work

Stress has often been cited in cases going to Tribunals and has led to substantial awards for employees who have resigned because they are not willing to endure it any longer. It is very difficult to define and many people **want** to have some pressure put on them.

You need to keep an eye on any team members who are perhaps trying to balance family commitments with working ones, or struggling to take on a new job and responsibilities seldom previously undertaken by someone from their group. You should ensure that they receive suitable support for a short period and take advice from your manager or the human resources department if what is required is outside your own authority to provide.

5.6 Implementing flexible working arrangements

In the case of the husband (described in Session B) who had asked for reduced hours to look after his baby, the employer did support family-friendly working practices generally, but felt unable to do so in the applicant's case. As the employer had helped four female employees but turned down the first man to ask, the Tribunal held it to be discriminatory.

The changing climate of employee relations

You need to be aware of both the changing laws and changing employee expectations on discrimination issues, for example the RMT union has negotiated an agreement with London Underground which includes the development of a framework to facilitate a work-lifestyle balance and family-friendly policies on behalf of its members who constitute a large proportion of the total workforce in a business which demands that much work is done at nights and at weekends.

Try to treat each request you receive on its real merits and not base your reactions on 'what we've always done before', because this may not be socially acceptable or legally justifiable in the future. Seek advice from your manager if for any reason you believe there could be a latent source of discontent in this area.

Self-assessment 5 ·   10 mins

1 Fill in the blanks in the following sentence.

Employees who believe that they have been _____ _____ against can apply to an _____ _____ without serving any _____ _____ period.

2 Name four potential adverse consequences of reinstatement, one each for:

■ the organization;
■ the team leader whose area is affected;
■ the other team members;
■ the person reinstated.

The organization

_____

The team leader whose area is affected

_____

The team members

_____

The person reinstated

_____

3 Fill in the blanks in the following sentence.

Tribunals can make _____ awards in respect of_____ _____, in addition to those made for direct loss of wages, salary or financial benefits.

4 Give four examples of practices which might be seen as bullying or harassment.

1 _____

2 _____

3 _____

4 _____

Fill in the blanks in the following sentences.

5 The consequences for a team leader complicit in acts of illegal discrimination could include _____ of_____ from team members,_____ _____ or loss of _____ _____ opportunities.

6 _____ of roles can lead to claims of _____ discrimination from members of groups who feel _____ from applying for them.

7 Word of mouth recruitment is an example of a recruitment practice which is likely to be seen as _____ _____.

8 Employment Tribunals are under no obligation to consider the _____ of _____ to _____ the compensation which they award.

9 The consequences for a company found guilty of illegal discrimination can include loss of _____ _____ and customer _____ as well as any direct financial penalties.

10 To convince an Employment Tribunal of your case you must be able to _____ that on the _____ of _____ the decision which you took is justified.

11 Name three things which, if mishandled by a local team leader, could lead to serious consequences under the equal opportunities legislation.

The answers to these questions can be found on pages 166–7.

6 Summary

- The consequences for transgressing illegal discrimination laws can be very serious for organizations and managers at all levels.

- For an organization, consequences include unlimited awards of compensation to victims, potentially running into hundreds of thousands of pounds or more.

- Tribunals do not consider the ability to pay of an employer, or the nature of its work.

- Awards made for hurt feelings are increasingly made and in some cases are akin to the punitive damages awarded in libel cases for loss of reputation.

  > In 2000, the average cost to employers of illegal discrimination settlements was more than £12,000 per case. This figure excludes legal costs which probably add up to £5,000 per case.

- Nearly 50% of awards made in discrimination cases are for hurt feelings.

- Managers can face disciplinary action or loss of promotional prospects for instigating, abetting or condoning illegal discrimination.

- First line managers need to be especially sensitive to behaviour that may be offensive to members of particular groups and which may amount to harassment.

- An aggrieved employee has rights under the legislation from 'day one'.

- Organizations can lose their local reputation, the morale of their workforce and the good will of their customers if found guilty of illegal discrimination – which will always be a big local news item.

- Some of the behaviour apparently condoned by managers in organizations taken to tribunals is so crass that it could represent gross misconduct worthy of summary dismissal.

- Team leaders and first line managers need to be sensitive to the changing climate of opinion which influences both employees' expectations and the reactions of Tribunals to illegal discrimination.

- The risk of serious consequences as the result of discrimination is real and can result from a very wide range of behaviours, some of which may stem from entrenched custom and practice in organizational or departmental culture.

Session F
Discipline

1 Introduction

Any group of people is much more effective when it works as a team. As a team leader in your own workplace you will no doubt appreciate that fact.

Without discipline, teamwork can easily break down. If individual members of a team are refusing to pull their weight or cannot perform to the standards required of them, then the overall effectiveness of the group suffers. Other members, seeing that they are doing more than their colleagues, will either decide to take it easy themselves, or become angry that work is not being shared evenly.

Remember, discipline is not about punishment. It is about resolving problems at work in as fair a manner as possible. In the interests of fairness, there should always be clear rules about the way that disciplinary problems are dealt with. In this Session we'll examine each of the stages in the process of maintaining discipline.

2 The purpose of discipline

This workbook concentrates on practical ways of handling discipline. However, before we start we should try to define what discipline is for.

Activity 44

Write down **two** purposes of discipline at work.

_____

_____

_____

_____

See whether you agree with the following arguments.

Discipline at work has four main objectives:

- safety;
- fairness;
- prosperity of the organization;
- compliance with a contract.

2.1 Safety

Someone entering a workplace for the first time won't necessarily be able to know how to behave. In particular, he or she probably won't be aware of the dangers of that workplace, and so won't be safe until told about the hazards and the means of protection against those hazards. Employees who ignore safety rules, or who indulge in fighting or drinking at work, for example, may endanger others.

2.2 Fairness

People may under-perform in various ways which impose extra work and responsibility on their colleagues. Sometimes this may be conduct such as lateness or absenteeism, but it may also be that they cannot meet the standards required for output or quality. Fairness must be seen to flow from the employer, evidenced by proper training or re-training, and from the first line manager through offering appropriate support. In return, individuals must observe the rules and ask for help if they cannot meet the standards set.

2.3 Prosperity of the organization

For an organization to prosper, it will need the vast majority of employees to obey the rules and meet the agreed performance standards for the greater part of the time. Employees who fall short in either respect should be given support and the opportunity to improve in whatever respect they are failing. For the few who cannot, or will not, improve, then the formal disciplinary procedures exist to offer a final series of opportunities to do so before they must be dismissed in the interests of their colleagues and the other stakeholders in the organization.

2.4 Compliance with a contract

Under the terms of the contract of employment, the employer provides facilities and resources, such as training, supervision and payment for agreed work done. In return, the employees commit themselves to meeting agreed standards of conduct and performance once their training is completed.

Discipline at work should work for the benefit of the organization and everyone who works in it.

And when dealing with a disciplinary offence, there is one guiding principle:

The main aim is improvement in performance, not punishment.

3 Rules

If there is to be discipline at work, there has to be a set of rules. Rules help to determine the standards of conduct expected from employees.

This is important because people need to know what is expected of them.

> **Everyone needs to know what the rules are, and the reasons for the rules.**

Activity 45

3 mins

Note down **two** or **three** examples of the rules that affect the people at your place of work.

_____

_____

_____

Typical of the kinds of rule that are found in work organizations are:

- rules about timekeeping;
- rules about absence;
- rules about health and safety;
- rules about using company facilities;
- rules about who does what;
- rules about what constitutes gross misconduct.

The law of the land applies at work as well as outside it, even though the list of rules drawn up by an organization won't normally remind employees of that fact. It goes without saying that it is a disciplinary offence to steal or to damage property, for instance.

It's obviously preferable for the rules of an organization to be written down.

Activity 46

4 mins

Even if the rules are written down, there can be problems in communicating the rules to all employees.

Note **one** such problem, and say how it could be overcome.

_____

_____

_____

_____

Problems can arise with:

- new employees, who aren't familiar with the accepted and safe ways to behave in the new workplace. They need to have the rules explained to them – it usually isn't good enough simply to provide a copy of the rules, especially where safety is concerned. Explaining the rules forms part of an induction programme;
- people who don't speak English as their first language. You must take steps to make sure the rules are understood. If you don't speak the particular language yourself, you will need help from more senior management or the human resources department to make sure you act effectively;
- young people, who don't have experience of working life. Again, it may fall to you to ensure that a young person fully understands the rules and why they have to be followed.

4 Dealing with offences

What is a disciplinary offence?

Activity 47

4 mins

Let's start by thinking about the disciplinary offences you may have had to deal with at work, or those you may have heard about.

Note down some examples of disciplinary offences. Try to think of **three** or **four**. An example is stealing.

_____

_____

_____

_____

Here are some disciplinary offences:

- fighting;
- verbal abuse;
- lateness;
- abusing company equipment;

- disobeying a reasonable instruction;
- stealing;
- smoking in a non-smoking area;
- horse-play.

You may have come up with offences not on this list. The list of disciplinary offences is as long as our imaginations can make it.

However, all these offences involve one thing:

all disciplinary matters involve a breach of rules or failure to meet agreed standards of work.

If we want to deal with disciplinary matters in a consistent and fair way, we need to:

- know what the standards and **rules** are; and
- have a well-designed **procedure** for implementing them.

Let's think about the steps a manager or team leader needs to take when there has been a suspected disciplinary offence.

Activity 48

Suppose someone in another team stops you in the corridor and says something like:

'Two of your blokes left an hour early last night. That's not the first time. I don't think it's fair. What are you going to do about it?'

What is the **first** thing you would do?

_____

_____

Perhaps you agree that the first thing to be done when a breach of the rules is reported is to:

find out the facts.

Until you've looked into the matter thoroughly to see if the accusation has any truth in it, you aren't in a position to make any judgements.

Activity 49

3 mins

What might you do next, assuming you found out that **two** of your work team had left early without permission?

_____

_____

_____

_____

You might do one of a number of things. You could for instance:

■ have a quiet word with them;
■ give them a warning about their behaviour;
■ take the matter further and start formal disciplinary proceedings.

Before taking the matter forward, you need to determine whether you have the necessary authority to act. If you haven't, or are not sure, it is imperative to consult your own manager before going too far along the disciplinary road.

Any formal procedures usually involve a **disciplinary interview**. This gives the people accused a chance to state their version of the facts. Then you would be able to come to a considered judgement about what penalty you should impose – if any.

Once you decided on the action to be taken, you'd need to record the information and keep an eye on things from that point on.

We can sum up all these steps in the form of a diagram. We'll be using this diagram as we go through the rest of this part of the workbook.

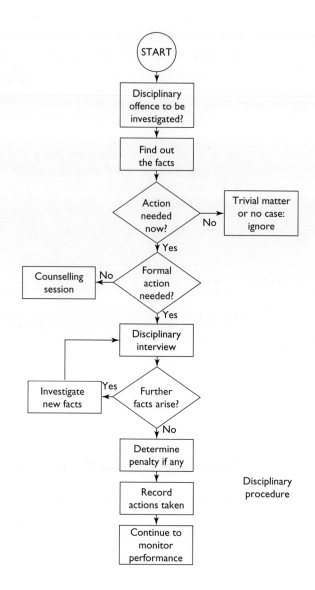

Disciplinary procedure

Activity 50

20 mins

I Explain how well you ensure that your team members are kept informed of the organization's disciplinary procedures.

_____

_____

_____

2 What actions do you intend to take to make them better informed? (Learn more yourself? Hold a team meeting? Talk to individuals? Or what other actions?)

_____

_____

_____

3 How confident are you that the contributions you make to implementing disciplinary and grievance procedures are consistent with your organization's values and policies?

_____

_____

_____

4 If you are less than totally confident about this, what actions will you take? (Talk to your manager? Talk to the Human Resources department? Some other action?)

_____

_____

_____

Record below the result of the actions taken in 2 and 4 above.

_____

_____

_____

_____

_____

_____

_____

5 Following the procedures

EXTENSIONS 9, 10, 11 and 12
ACAS has produced several useful publications on disciplinary and grievance procedures.

As all organizations have to cope with disciplinary problems, most of them have developed systematic procedures for handling them.

A **disciplinary procedure** is a set of written guidelines to help everyone at work – managers, team leaders, other employees and shop stewards – to deal with disciplinary matters.

Activity 51

5 mins

Imagine that a member of your team is failing to meet the standards set for output performance and quality. In your opinion, it is a serious matter and has continued for some time despite informal approaches from you. It merits a first written warning.

How would you act if the team member concerned were:

A long-serving employee, with a previously unblemished record

_____

_____

A shop steward

_____

_____

An employee who has had other written warnings, all now time-expired, for unrelated matters

_____

_____

A young employee who is your second cousin

_____

_____

An employee of West Indian or Irish origin

_____

_____

Your answer should be that you would act the same way in any of the situations described, based on your assessment of the facts.

To appear fair to an Employment Tribunal, the procedures must be implemented in a consistent way. Everyone must be treated in the same way for the same offence – and all team leaders and managers must act in the same way whatever department they work in.

It makes a great deal of sense to make notes of what is said and done for future reference. Tell people that you will be doing so, and explain that you are doing it simply to ensure that there is an accurate record of what has been said. This will be to everyone's benefit.

The following extracts from an example of a good disciplinary procedure is taken with permission from *Discipline at Work – The ACAS Advisory Handbook* and reflects the ACAS Code of Practice relating to disciplinary practice and procedures in employment.

5.1 Sound procedures

(1) Purpose and scope

This procedure is designed to help and encourage all employees to achieve and maintain standards of conduct, attendance and job performance. The company rules (a copy of which is displayed in the office) and this procedure apply to all employees. The aim is to ensure consistent and fair treatment for all.

Notice that the procedure starts by stating:

- **what** the procedure is for;
- **where** the procedure can be seen;
- **to whom** it applies.

(2) Principles

a) No disciplinary action will be taken against an employee until the case has been fully investigated.

b) At every stage in the procedure the employee will be advised of the nature of the complaint against him or her and will be given the opportunity to state his or her case before any decision is made.

c) At all stages the employee will have the right to be accompanied by a shop steward, employee representative or work colleague during the disciplinary interview.

Activity 52

Why is it good practice to allow someone who is under investigation to be represented by a union official or a colleague?

_____

_____

_____

_____

As you may have answered, having a union official or a friend of the alleged offender present can help to ensure there is 'fair play', and that the case is fully understood by the individual.

To continue with the ACAS example procedure:

d) No employee will be dismissed for the first breach of discipline except in the case of gross misconduct when the penalty will be dismissal without notice or payment in lieu of notice.

(We'll discuss what is meant by 'gross misconduct' shortly.)

e) An employee will have the right to appeal against any disciplinary penalty imposed.
f) The procedure may be implemented at any stage if the employee's alleged misconduct warrants such action.

Activity 53

Point (e) above is another 'essential ingredient' of a good disciplinary procedure.

Can you think of **one** reason why it is so important to allow an appeal against a penalty?

_____

_____

You may agree that allowing the right of appeal:

- helps to make sure that justice is done;
- reduces the possibility that someone will be harshly punished due to personal bias or animosity;
- in the case of a dispute over the decision, allows fresh minds to be brought in.

Now we come to the main part of the procedure (which we looked at briefly in Session A). Read the following extract carefully and note that:

- There are a number of stages. (As was stated in the principles above, the procedure may be entered at any stage – it doesn't have to be followed step by step.)
- Each stage is a more serious step than the one before.

(3) The Procedure

Minor faults will be dealt with informally but where the matter is more serious the following procedure will be used:

Stage 1 – Oral warning

If conduct or performance does not meet acceptable standards the employee will normally be given a formal **oral warning**. He or she will be advised of the reason for the warning, that it is the first stage of the disciplinary procedure and of his or her right of appeal. A brief note of the oral warning will be kept but will be spent after . . . months, subject to satisfactory conduct and performance.

Stage 2 – Written warning

If the offence is a serious one, or if a further offence occurs, a **written warning** will be given to the employee by the first line manager. This will give details of the complaint, the improvement required and the timescale. It will warn that action under Stage 3 will be considered if there is no satisfactory improvement and will advise of the right of appeal. A copy of this written warning will be kept by the first line manager but it will be disregarded for disciplinary purposes after . . . months subject to satisfactory conduct and performance.

Stage 3 – Final written warning or disciplinary suspension

If there is still a failure to improve and conduct or performance is still unsatisfactory, or if the misconduct is sufficiently serious to warrant only one written warning but insufficiently serious to justify dismissal (in effect both first and final written warning), a **final written warning** will normally be given to the employee. This will give details of the complaint, will warn that dismissal will result if there is no satisfactory improvement and will advise of the right of appeal. A copy of this final written warning will be kept by the first line manager but it will be spent after . . . months (in exceptional cases the period may be longer) subject to satisfactory conduct and performance.

Alternatively, consideration will be given to imposing a penalty of a disciplinary suspension without pay for up to a maximum of five working days.

Stage 4 – Dismissal

If conduct or performance is still unsatisfactory and the employee still fails to reach the prescribed standards, **dismissal** will normally result. Only the appropriate senior manager can take the decision to dismiss. The employee will be provided, as soon as reasonably practicable, with written reasons for dismissal, the date on which employment will terminate and the right of appeal.

Activity 54 · 4 mins

Answer the following questions about the procedure above by circling the appropriate box.

		YES	NO
1	Would every minor offence have to be taken through the procedure above?	YES	NO

2 In which stages do the warnings given become spent or disregarded after a period of time?

| 1 | 2 | 3 | 4 |

3 After which stages does the employee have a right of appeal?

| 1 | 2 | 3 | 4 |

4 At which stages are the warnings written down?

| 1 | 2 | 3 | 4 |

5 At which stages does the employee receive a written document?

| 1 | 2 | 3 | 4 |

The answers to this activity can be found on page 169.

Now let's deal with what is meant by 'gross misconduct'.

Activity 55

Stealing would be classified as 'gross misconduct'. List **four** other disciplinary offences that you would expect to come into this category.

_____

_____

_____

_____

Let's see what ACAS suggest as examples of offences normally regarded as gross misconduct:

- theft, fraud or deliberate falsification of records;
- fighting, or assault on another person;
- deliberate damage to company property;
- serious incapability through alcohol or being under the influence of illegal drugs;
- serious negligence which causes unacceptable loss, damage or injury;
- serious acts of insubordination.

There isn't always universal agreement about what constitutes gross misconduct, and your organization may have different ideas.

One survey of British companies and local authorities found that gambling was considered by different organizations to be:

- a minor disciplinary offence;
- a major disciplinary offence;
- gross misconduct.

The procedure that we have discussed is just one example of a disciplinary procedure that could be used by an organization, and is intended as a model for a company writing its own procedure.

> **Your own organization will probably have its own procedure. That's the one you have to follow.**

6 Finding out the facts

The start of our disciplinary procedure diagram shows the first step to be taken:

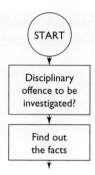

Read the following case and then think about what further information you would need.

Activity 56 · 5 mins

Mrs Jones, who works in the offices at her company, one day spends some time going round the other staff collecting money for a local hospital.

Those are all the facts as you know them. You are asked to decide whether Mrs Jones has committed a disciplinary offence by doing this.

What other information would you need to know, before making your judgement?

Jot down **four** questions you would ask.

_____

_____

_____

_____

Your questions may be included here.

- ■ How long did Mrs Jones take to make her collection?
- ■ What prompted her to do it?

- Has she or anyone else in the organization done this sort of thing before?
- Is there a well-known management rule about what she did?
- Is Mrs Jones's general record a good one?
- Is it important that she did not leave her desk?
- Did she get permission to make the collection?

When we find out the answers to these kind of questions, it becomes possible to decide about the case.

Here are two possible sets of circumstances.

Activity 57

6 mins

Mrs Jones works in the wages department. On Monday morning, she cleared up her work, and then went round her colleagues in the department to collect money for the purchase of equipment at a local hospital. She made this collection during an extended coffee break, taking about 45 minutes in all. The first person Mrs Jones collected from was her office first line manager. Everybody in the office knew that Mrs Jones's husband had been treated for cancer at the local hospital. It was also true that other people had collected for charities in the past.

Is this a disciplinary offence?
YES   NO

What (briefly) are the reasons for your decision?

_____

_____

_____

Mrs Jones works as a receptionist at a local company. One Wednesday morning she repeatedly left the reception area unattended while visiting other offices to collect money. One way and another, the collection had taken most of the morning. Mrs Jones tried to keep well clear of the office manager. She was collecting for the sports and social fund at the hospital where her husband works. She also collects every week for the football pools, and management had already warned her about the time she was taking on this.

Is this a disciplinary offence?   YES   NO

What (briefly) are the reasons for your decision?

_____

_____

_____

Compare your answers with the response given on page 170.

The discussion following this Activity leads to the conclusion that:

it is important to make sure that as much relevant information as possible is collected about each case.

It is also important that this is done promptly, before memories of the incident fade.

One formula that can help us collect information thoroughly is the '5W' formula.

6.1 The 5W formula

This formula consists of five questions:

WHO?	WHEN?	WHAT?	WHERE?	WHY?

Let's look at them one at a time.

■ **Who?**

Disciplinary offences always involve people so we need to ask:

- **Who** was involved?
- **Who** were the witnesses?
- **Who** are the first line managers involved?
- **Who** is the trade union representative?

■ **When?**

It is always important to know when an incident happened. A whole argument can be destroyed if the wrong time or day is written down. For example, if the incident is mistakenly thought to have taken place on a Wednesday afternoon, and then the person under investigation is subsequently able to prove he or she was somewhere else at the time, the whole case collapses.

It is especially important to know whether the incident happened inside or outside working hours.

■ **What?**

Before any action can be contemplated, it is obviously vital to know exactly what happened. This is seldom as easy as it sounds. In many disciplinary cases there are likely to be different versions of the same event, especially where the misconduct is serious enough for dismissal. This is where your judgement comes in.

■ **Where?**

Establishing where a disciplinary offence took place is important for the record. For instance, smoking may be allowed in the canteen, but not on the petrol station forecourt. If one of your team commits an offence in another section, another first line manager may have to be involved in the investigation.

■ **Why?**

The final question is to ask why the incident took place. The answer to this can make the difference between whether it is treated as a disciplinary case or not.

In asking **why,** we should remember two things:

- why did the incident happen at that time or place?
- why did it involve that particular person?

Activity 58

The Cartwheel Company is a medium-sized firm operating three shifts. The shop floor is divided into a number of different sections, and normally two first line managers are on the night shift.

For two weeks now, one first line manager has been off sick and no proper cover has been arranged. Towards the end of the night shift, Harry Davies, one of the shop floor engineers, goes to see the only first line manager available. He complains that some of the men in his unit have set up a card school, and that they are never back from breaks on time. Harry claims to represent at least four other men in the section who are all fed up with carrying the extra work created by the others never being there on time.

Use the **who**, **when**, **what**, **where** and **why** formula to investigate this matter.

Write down the questions you would want answers to, in the space below.

Who? _____

_____

When? _____

_____

What? _____

_____

Where? _____

_____

Why? _____

_____

The following are typical questions drawn out by the 5W formula:

Who?

- **Who** were the members of the alleged card school?
- **Who** were those Harry said he represents?
- **Who** were the witnesses?
- **Who** were the first line managers?
- **Who** is the trade union representative?

When?

- **When** did the alleged card school sessions take place – dates and times?
- **When** did they start and finish – dates and times?

What?

- **What** did the card school involve? (Gambling for money, or was it just for fun?)
- **What** extra work did Harry and his colleagues have to do?
- **What** is the past record of this kind of offence?

Where?

- **Where** did the card school take place? (In the canteen? On the shop floor?)

Why?

- **Why** has Harry come to you? (Has he a personal grudge which has led him to blow up a small incident out of all proportion?)
- **Why** are the card games taking place? (Is the work badly organized?)
- **Why** has the information come to you in this way? (Does supervision need to be improved?)

I hope you agree with me that the 5W formula has succeeded in raising most of the important questions about the case.

Nevertheless, when you are investigating an incident like this, you will need continually to ask yourself:

is there anything more I need to know?

7 The counselling session

Let's remind ourselves of the first part of our procedure diagram for dealing with an alleged disciplinary offence:

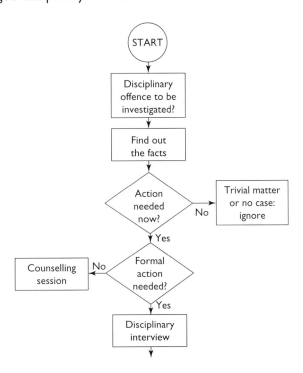

Once we have found out the facts of the case, we should know whether a disciplinary offence has been committed.

The question then arises:

Is action needed at this time?

If your judgement is that action is needed, there is another decision to be made:

Is it more appropriate to 'have a quiet word' with the offender, or is the offence serious enough to warrant a disciplinary interview?

Later in this section, we'll look into the disciplinary interview. For the moment, let's examine what's involved in a counselling session or informal discussion.

As a team leader, you are concerned to get a good performance from each member of your team, which means that breaches of discipline cannot be tolerated for long. However, you have an important role in supporting your team members. An informal discussion is an opportunity to offer your support if it is needed. If a person is under-performing, it could be due to stress and personal difficulties. A friendly approach from you can mean a lot to a harassed employee.

> Geoff Parks had been a first line manager for three years and his work-team hadn't changed much during that time.
>
> One morning, Geoff saw Jed Tarrow, one of his team, walking across the yard. He noticed Jed wasn't wearing a safety helmet.
>
> The next time Geoff saw Jed, they were both queuing at the staff canteen for lunch. They exchanged greetings and talked a while about a job Jed was working on. Then Geoff said:
>
> 'I noticed you in the yard yesterday without a helmet, Jed. That's very unlike you.'
>
> 'Sorry about that, boss. I was thinking about something else – don't know what made me forget.'
>
> 'You won't let it happen again, will you Jed? I look to you to set an example.'

You may deal with some minor breaches of discipline in a similar way yourself. Geoff knew that it would be enough to give Jed a gentle reminder. To have mentioned disciplinary procedures would not have helped here.

Compare this with the next case.

> Lila Podesta was a bright but unpredictable young woman. She worked in a large dress shop and, because she had a flair for it, the manager, Hilda Grace, allowed her to do most of the window dressing. Lila knew she

was good at this and had jokingly threatened to take her talents elsewhere if Hilda criticized her work in any way.

However, Lila 'took advantage' of her situation by repeatedly arriving to work late. Finally Hilda knew she'd have to do something. When Lila arrived one morning, half an hour late, she invited her into the office. This is what she said:

'Lila, I have a problem. Several of the other girls have complained to me that you are late to work every day, and I do nothing about it. What do you think I should do?'

'Tell me off, I suppose.'

'Lila, you are good at your job, but I think you are letting yourself down. I don't want to lose you, but wherever you work people won't put up with persistent lateness. Is there a particular problem at home?'

'Not really.'

'Well, we all have a job to do. I know that the company management won't allow me to take no action for very long. I have to ask you, to be fair to everyone else working here, to make an effort and get to work on time.'

Hilda knew that this was all she could do before invoking formal disciplinary procedures. She also knew that, if she did that, Lila would probably leave. It's the kind of difficult situation which you might have to deal with from time to time.

The rules are made for everyone. If someone breaks them, then sooner or later you have to take action.

Respect and confidentiality

One important aspect of dealing with disciplinary matters is that everyone deserves to be treated with respect, whether or not you believe them to have broken the rules.

Furthermore, all conversations between you and an individual regarding that person's conduct should be kept confidential. You may have to pass on information to those with a need to know it – your manager, perhaps, or the Human Resources department – but a breach of discipline is not something that should normally be discussed with other team members.

In many work situations, confidentiality can be difficult to maintain. When a group of people work closely together, for example, any unusual event may lead to speculation and gossip. The team leader plays a key role here, in:

■ making it clear that information and views given in confidence are not for general consumption;

■ setting an example by not joining in gossip about team members or other colleagues;

■ not, under normal circumstances, discussing the behaviour of one team member with another;

■ if possible, putting a halt to gossip by providing clear-cut information, but without disclosing anything that is not the concern of those not directly involved.

Fine lines must sometimes be trod. It is worth remembering that what counts above everything is the way the team leader behaves. If he or she can earn the respect of the team, and they know that their leader is incorruptible and trustworthy in all things, problems of this kind will tend not to arise.

Activity 59

Here are two sets of self-searching questions for you.

S/NVQ B11

1 When dealing with matters of discipline, are you scrupulous in treating individuals with respect, whatever their suspected misdemeanour?

_____

Do you feel that others in your organization always maintain respect for the individual during disciplinary interviews and the like?

_____

Explain in what way, if at all, you intend to modify your approach in this regard. If you need evidence for your S/NVQ portfolio, you should:

■ describe one or more particular incidents in the past in some detail (omitting the names of individuals if you wish), which you thought were not handled well;

■ explain in detail how you will modify your disciplinary procedures, so that anyone accused of a disciplinary offence is treated with proper respect;

■ explain how you intend to ensure that your modified procedures will be followed. (For example, you may decide to discuss your proposals with someone from the Human Resources department, and invite them to monitor your disciplinary interviews.)

_____

_____

_____

_____

2   Does gossip tend to be rife among your team members, especially when something occurs that requires disciplinary action to be taken?

_____

_____

Explain how you usually deal with this kind of problem.

_____

_____

Now explain what you think you might do differently in this regard in the future. Again, for portfolio evidence, you must be very specific about the changes you will make, and your proposed method for ensuring these changes are followed.

_____

_____

_____

_____

_____

_____

8 Taking action

Once it is decided that formal action is to be taken, a disciplinary interview must take place.

From the procedure diagram we can see the stages to be followed:

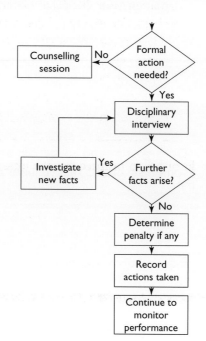

8.1 The purpose of an interview

The purposes of a disciplinary interview are to:

- allow the employee to give his or her version of the incident;
- ensure a full discussion, so that everyone present has a chance to hear the facts and to present any new facts;
- advise the employee of his or her rights;
- enable a fair judgement to be made so that an appropriate penalty can be imposed.

Before the interview, we have to **prepare.**

8.2 Preparing for the interview

Let's remind ourselves of the case we looked at earlier.

The Cartwheel Company is a medium-sized firm operating three shifts. The shop floor is divided into a number of different sections, and normally two first line managers are on the night shift.

For two weeks now, one first line manager has been off sick and no proper cover has been arranged. Towards the end of the night shift, Harry Davies, one of the shop floor engineers, goes to see the only first line manager available. He complains that some of the men in his unit have set up a card school, and that they are never back from breaks on time. Harry claims to represent at least four other men in the section who are all fed up with carrying the extra work created by the others never being there on time.

In order to prepare for the interview, we can apply our '5W' formula once more.

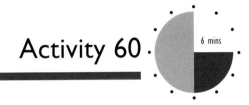

Activity 60

6 mins

Use the 5W formula by answering each of the following questions. You only need give **one** answer to each question.

What is the meeting about?

_____

_____

Why do we need this meeting?

_____

_____

Who should be at the meeting?

_____

_____

Where should the meeting take place?

_____

_____

When should the meeting take place?

_____

_____

Compare your answers with the following.

- **What** is the meeting about?

  It is alleged that a card school has been started.

- **Why** do we need this meeting?

  Because this could well be a disciplinary offence.

- **Who** should be at the meeting?

  - Witnesses – to confirm the truth of the report.

  - Perhaps other first line managers – to find out what they know or may have already done.

  - The union representative – to keep them in the picture, and to represent the people being accused.

  - The person or persons accused of the offence.

- **Where** should the meeting take place?

  A quiet area away from the workplace is much more likely to result in a satisfactory interview than a noisy area, or where others might overhear.

- **When** should the meeting take place?

  We need to give everyone involved time to prepare for the interview, so we shouldn't rush into it. We may also need to check on when the participants are available, and what times might cause the minimum disruption of work.

8.3 The interview

The interview is something that nobody looks forward to. This is all the more reason for handling it absolutely by the book.

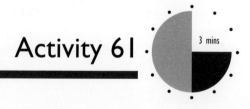

Activity 61

3 mins

How should an interview begin?

_____

_____

_____

_____

Like any other kind of meeting, an interview should start by introducing the people present and saying what the purpose of the meeting is.

> The person alleged to be the leading member of the card school at the Cartwheel Company is called Ray Cooley. Ray has been asked to attend the interview so that we can hear what he's got to say, and eventually determine what further action should be taken.

Compare the following two ways of starting the interview:

1 The first line manager meets Ray on the shop floor.

   'Look here, Ray, I know you're running a card school, so don't deny it. Nobody's getting any work done in your section and I'm sick to the back teeth with complaints. I'm giving you a written warning. Now get back to work.'

2 The first line manager arranges the interview in an office. The shop steward is present.

   'Sit yourself down, Ray. You've been asked to come along today because it has been reported that you have been running a card school during the firm's time. I've checked it out and it seems you are involved, so I've called you in to have a chat about it. I think you know the other people here. You know that playing cards during working hours is against company rules, so let's hear what you've got to say.'

> However angry you may feel, it's important not to lose your temper. If you do, your behaviour could be considered in law as unreasonable.

The first approach is likely to put Ray's back up and lead to conflict.

The second approach is much more likely to be profitable. It encourages Ray to talk and shows that no one has prejudged the case.

A courteous but firm manner is needed. It is important to encourage the employee to talk about the offence.

During the interview, it is best not to make any decisions straight away, especially where the case is a serious one.

Give yourself time to think. Adjourn the interview before you come to a conclusion.

And, most importantly:

keep a cool head – don't get emotionally involved.

8.4 The decision

Eventually a decision must be made.

Activity 62

2 mins

What procedure should be used to decide the further action to be taken?

Look on page 170 for feedback to this Activity.

This is how one first line manager could have ended his interview with our alleged card player, Ray Cooley.

> 'Right, Ray, this is the last time I want to see you in here. I'll get to the bottom of this card school affair and you'll end up being disciplined. I'm warning you not to get involved again. That's my decision, and it's final, so get out of my office.'

Activity 63

4 mins

Bearing in mind what the first line manager is supposed to be doing here, how many things can you find wrong with the statement above?

_____

_____

_____

_____

You may have noticed a number of problems with this first line manager's approach. Perhaps they are included here.

- It is not clear what decision – if any – has been made.
- It is not clear what sort of warning Ray has been given.

- The first line manager hasn't asked the union (or other) representative to comment.
- It is not clear what the first line manager is going to do next.
- Ray hasn't been told of his right to appeal.
- Ray hasn't been asked to respond to the statement.

I hope you agree that there are better ways to end interviews.

Such an end to a disciplinary meeting would be very unhelpful, to say the least, if the facts of it were ever to appear to before an Employment Tribunal.

Activity 64

5 mins

Read through this account of another first line manager talking to Ray Cooley, and note down the good points.

First line manager:	Right, Ray, let's just sum up then. You admit that on three separate occasions – we've got the dates here – you were involved in a card school during working time. You also know that was against the work rules. Do you agree?
Ray:	Yes.
Shop steward:	Agreed.
First line manager:	You understand that under the agreed procedure, I can give you a verbal warning for a first offence, and that is what I intend to do. Do you accept that, Ray?
Ray:	Fair enough.
Shop steward:	That seems fair if it's consistent with what happened to the others.
First line manager:	Yes, you've been involved in all the cases, so we know we are being consistent.
	OK, Ray, so this is an official verbal warning which will be confirmed to me by your union and the Human Resources department. This is the first stage of the company's disciplinary procedure. It will stay on record for six months – that will take us to the 15th of August – and if there are no more problems we will wipe the slate clean then.
	If you do offend again, you should be aware that this will lead to further stages of the disciplinary procedure, and may eventually result in your being

dismissed. You do have a right of appeal against this penalty, and if you want to do so, you should let Mr Renwick know by Friday.

Any final questions?

Note down the good points.

_____

_____

_____

_____

_____

Look on pages 170–1 for feedback on this activity.

8.5 After the interview

It may be tempting to heave a sigh of relief and put the matter behind you, but it is very important to complete the process thoroughly.

Activity 65

What more is there to be done, following the disciplinary interview?

_____

_____

_____

Remember the last part of our procedure diagram:

↓ No

Determine
penalty if any

↓

Record
actions taken

↓

Continue to
monitor
performance

You can see that there are two more main actions:

■ to write down the actions which have been taken

It is the job of the person holding the interview to record what took place. In some workplaces, the Human Resources department may take on this task.

■ to continue to monitor the behaviour of the person penalized for the offence

If the employee is in your team, it will be your job to keep an eye on the team member.

Let's summarize the main points to remember for the whole process.

■ **Prepare** by:

  ■ making sure you have all the information you will need;
  ■ letting everyone involved know when and where the interview is to be held;
  ■ giving the employee time to prepare.

■ **At the interview:**

  ■ introduce everyone present, explaining why they are there;
  ■ allow the employee to state his or her case;
  ■ keep the tone of the interview formal but courteous – don't lose your temper;
  ■ consider adjourning the interview to give time for a considered decision;
  ■ explain clearly what decision has been made and what further action is to be taken.

■ **After the interview:**

  ■ record the action taken;
  ■ continue to monitor the situation.

Records must be complete and accurate. According to ACAS, records should include:

■ details of the nature of any breach of disciplinary rules;
■ the action taken and the reasons for it;
■ whether an appeal was lodged;
■ its outcome and any subsequent developments.

These records should be carefully safeguarded and kept confidential.

Except in agreed special circumstances, breaches of disciplinary rules should be disregarded after a specified period of satisfactory conduct.

Remember that, if you keep records about individuals on computer, you may be subject to the Data Protection Act 1998. This obliges data users to register with the Data Protection Commissioner if the data they keep fall within the Act; failure to do this can lead to a large fine. The intent of the Act is to protect information about individuals, and to set up a mechanism whereby people can have access to information held about them.

8.6 Custom and practice

Read through the following short case study and think of yourself as being Petra Williams.

> Petra Williams was about to take over as team leader in a busy warehouse. She was being shown around by her predecessor, Tony. At one point, he warned her to 'get out of the road' as a fork lift truck approached at high speed.
>
> 'That truck shouldn't be going at that speed – there's an 8 mph speed limit in here', she said.
>
> Tony smiled. 'Not on Friday afternoons there isn't', he said. 'It's "POETS" day: "push off early, tomorrow's Saturday". Everyone wants to be away by four o'clock – we've always worked that way to keep everyone sweet.'

Activity 66

3 mins

This is one example of 'custom and practice' at work, something which can be very hard to change and which is often quoted as a reason for breaking the rules. Can you think of three examples from your own working experience, especially something you may have been involved with before you were promoted? Examples might be:

- using company equipment, such as faxes, telephones and email, for private use without permission;

- borrowing equipment (drills, sanders, power saws, cameras, lap top computers) over the weekend;

- carrying unauthorized materials or pets in company vehicles;

■ clocking (or signing) colleagues in to cover for lateness.

_____

_____

_____

As a team leader, you are best placed to know what actually happens and must be prepared to act at an early stage to prevent breaches of the rules becoming built in to the way people expect to work.

If unauthorized activities are allowed to become custom and practice, it will be much harder for you to eliminate them later. For example, imagine that the card school at the Cartwheel Company had been going for months, with managers 'turning a blind eye'; it would be much harder to take action about it.

In situations where serious or deep seated 'custom and practice' exists you will need to be tactful and may need help from your own manager or the Human Resources department.

Activity 67

15 mins

Are the records you keep concerning disciplinary matters always complete and accurate?	YES	NO
Do they always include details of the nature of any breach of disciplinary rules?	YES	NO
Do they always record the action taken and the reasons for it?	YES	NO
Do they always indicate whether an appeal was lodged?	YES	NO
Do they always note the outcome and subsequent developments?	YES	NO
Are the records always carefully safeguarded and kept confidential?	YES	NO

If you answered NO to any of the questions above, explain in what way your records are deficient, or have been in the past. (For S/NVQ portfolio evidence, you should produce copies of your records if possible.)

_____

_____

_____

_____

Your organization is registered with the Information Commissioner to hold these records?

YES	NO	Don't know

Now write down any actions you plan to take as a result of your answers to these questions, to ensure that your disciplinary records conform both to the ACAS recommendations and to your organization's legal requirements. For S/NVQ portfolio evidence, you should write out very specific plans, and show how these will help your records conform. At the first opportunity, a copy of your new improved records should be included.

_____

_____

_____

_____

_____

It may not be your job to keep disciplinary records, or to ensure conformity with the law. But if your team members are involved, you will no doubt want to know that proper records are being kept, and you may be expected to input information into those records.

Self-assessment 6

15 mins

1   Name one thing that all disciplinary offences involve.

_____

2   If a disciplinary offence is minor, a first line manager might decide that beginning the formal disciplinary procedure is unnecessary. What else might they do in this case?

_____

_____

3   Who benefits from there being clear rules for dealing with disciplinary offences?

_____

_____

4   Imagine that you have investigated a case and decided that formal action needs to be taken. Now you have to prepare for and hold a disciplinary interview.

     Here is a list of possible actions you might take. Pick out **seven** actions from the list and place them in the correct order, so as to describe an appropriate sequence of actions to be taken.

     a   Decide what penalty should be imposed.

     b   Decide where the meeting is to be held.

     c   Hold a counselling session.

     d   Continue to monitor performance.

     e   Decide who should be present.

     f   Introduce the participants, and state why they are there.

     g   Decide whether the case is serious enough for formal action.

     h   Sum up what's been said.

     i   Give the employee a chance to state his or her case.

_____

_____

Answers to these questions can be found on page 167.

9 Summary

- The actions involved in dealing with a disciplinary offence are:

  - find out the **facts**;
  - decide whether action is needed;
  - decide between formal action and informal action.

- If formal action is needed:

  - hold a disciplinary interview;
  - if further facts arise, investigate them;
  - determine penalty to be imposed, if any;
  - record the actions taken;
  - continue to monitor performance.

- An offence involves a breach of the rules or failure to meet standards for individual performance.

- Every well run sizeable organization should have a written disciplinary procedure.

- First line managers should always follow procedures when dealing with discipline.

- Records about disciplinary matters must be complete and accurate. They should include: details of breach of disciplinary rules; the action taken and the reasons for it; whether an appeal was lodged; its outcome and any subsequent developments.

  These records should be carefully safeguarded and kept confidential, and may be subject to the requirements of the Data Protection Act 1998.

- To bear scrutiny by an Employment Tribunal procedures must be applied consistently to all employees within a department and by managers across all departments in the organization.

Performance checks

1 Quick quiz

Jot down answers to the following questions on *Managing the Employment Relationship*.

Question 1   Why is it necessary to manage diversity in the workplace?

Question 2   'Inequality at work occurs when a person or group is treated in a less favourable way than others in the same situation.' What is the important word missing from this statement?

_____

_____

Question 3   If you suspected that there was a case of unlawful discrimination occurring in your work team, what is the first thing you would do?

_____

_____

Question 4   If, at work, one group is treated differently from another but nobody seems to have suffered any disadvantage, do you think it is likely that an offence has been committed?

_____

_____

Question 5   '*The Sex Discrimination Act* is designed specifically to protect women in employment.' Is this correct?

_____

_____

Question 6   What do we mean by the phrase **direct discrimination**?

_____

_____

Question 7   What do we mean by **indirect discrimination**?

_____

_____

Question 8   What do the letters **GOQ** stand for?

_____

_____

Question 9   What is meant by the word **victimization**, in terms of discrimination law?

_____

_____

Question 10   'You aren't allowed in law to instruct someone to discriminate unfairly but, if you are an employee and you are told to discriminate against someone then you can't be held responsible. After all, you were only doing your job.' Do you agree with this statement?

_____

_____

Question 11   Describe in your own words what is meant by the phrase **positive action**.

_____

_____

Question 12   What do you think an employer has to have done if he is to take no responsibility for an act of unlawful discrimination by one of his employees?

_____

_____

Question 13   Why is it important to keep records to show what steps have been taken to prevent discrimination in the workplace?

_____

_____

Question 14   Name two things which can be done to ensure that only relevant factors are taken into account when selecting people for jobs, promotion and so on.

_____

_____

Question 15   What do we mean by a **stereotype**?

_____

_____

Question 16   'This workbook has shown that equality concerns the following disadvantaged groups: women, racial minorities, the disabled and the elderly.' What is wrong with this statement?

_____

_____

Question 17   What is the upper limit of compensation which can be made to an employee found by a Tribunal to have been illegally discriminated against on the grounds of race, sex or disability?

_____

_____

Question 18   How does reinstatement differ from re-employment?

_____

_____

Question 19   Fill in the blanks in the following sentence.

Discrimination on the basis of _____, _____, _____ and _____ _____ are being considered as possible additional aspects of illegal discrimination.

Question 20   In cases of illegal discrimination, the applicant must serve at least 12 months with the employer before applying to a Tribunal.

TRUE/FALSE

Question 21   Name four items which a first line manager or team leader can control directly, or influence, to avoid adverse consequences arising from claims of illegal discrimination.

_____

Question 22   Which two documents covering the relationship between employers and employees must conform with the employment laws?

_____

_____

Question 23   What steps may the law expect an employer to take to ensure that an individual employee understands the procedures that apply to his or her employment?

_____

_____

Question 24   Suggest three ways in which employees might break their contract of employment other than through 'gross misconduct'.

_____

_____

Question 25   What action may employees take if they believe that they have been dismissed unfairly?

_____

_____

Question 26   What rights does a recognized trade union have on behalf of its members in a disciplinary situation?

_____

_____

Question 27   Why is it important to have an appeals procedure in grievance procedures?

_____

_____

Question 28   What are the letters 'ACAS' an abbreviation for?

_____

_____

Question 29   Why is it so important, legally speaking, to maintain accurate, up-to-date records of all matters affecting an individual's performance and conduct at work?

_____

_____

Question 30   There are four main objectives of discipline at work. Name **three** of them.

_____

_____

Question 31   There are four suggested stages of a disciplinary procedure, each stage requiring a stronger action than the last. Name three of them.

_____

_____

_____

Question 32   List **three** offences that would normally be considered as constituting 'gross misconduct'.

_____

_____

_____

Question 33   We discussed four purposes of a disciplinary interview. List **three** of these.

_____

_____

_____

Answers to these questions can be found on pages 171–3.

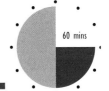

2 Workbook assessment

Read the following description and then answer the questions below, writing your answers on a separate sheet of paper.

> Dmitri, a Greek immigrant worker, has considerable problems speaking and understanding any but very simple English. When he took up his job as an operator in a factory, he was given no real induction by his team leader, John Ross, who left it to an English worker to start him off.

Dmitri failed to cope with the machinery he had to use. He was therefore moved to very low-level work with people from his own cultural group only. As a result, he learned very little English, and his problems of communication and understanding became even worse. The group of immigrants with whom he was working did not give him much help — indeed the team leader complained they were always fighting each other.

Then Dmitri caused a major accident as a result of not following the safety instructions he had been given in the factory's health and safety booklet, which every employee received on joining. The shop steward demanded his dismissal, claiming that Dmitri, like all new workers, had been shown proper safety procedures when he first took up his job. Evans, the steward, said that Dmitri was 'too thick to take anything in', and that he spent most of his time sulking and complaining instead of getting on with the work. He was a liability, and would have to go.

Soon after this, Dmitri came to Ross pleading for his job. He said that no one had ever explained the safety procedure to him, and that if he lost his job it would cause great hardship to his family. The team leader, however, feared that if he did not sack Dmitri, then the union and the English workers would create an uproar — there might even be a strike.

The company does not have an active equal opportunity policy, and although the team leader has an uneasy feeling that he'll have to watch his step here, he doesn't really know whether inequality of treatment has occurred; whether, if it has, it has been lawful; and how to respond to Evans's demand.

You need only write **one** or **two** sentences against each of the following questions.

1 How can Ross decide whether inequality of treatment has occurred here, and, if it has, whether it is lawful?

2 What should Ross say to Evans now?

3 Should the immigrant worker be disciplined or dismissed?

4 What could have been done to improve the induction given to Dmitri when he first took up a job in the factory?

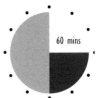

60 mins

3 Work-based assignment

S/NVQ
B11

The time guide for this assignment gives you an approximate idea of how long it is likely to take you to write up your findings. You will find you need to spend some additional time gathering information, perhaps talking to colleagues and thinking about the assignment. The result of your efforts should be presented on separate sheets of paper.

Your written response to this assignment may provide the basis of appropriate evidence for your S/NVQ portfolio.

What you have to do

1   Obtain a copy of your organization's policy on equal opportunities for all employees and potential employees, and compare it with the example given in this workbook (Extension 4).

■ Is your organization's policy applicable to all the groups which the law seeks to protect?
■ Are any other groups who might experience discrimination excluded from the policy?
■ How could your organization's equal opportunities policy be revised?

2   How is this policy communicated both internally and externally? Recommend any changes which you think are necessary.

3   In your opinion, what is potentially the most sensitive area of discrimination within your section? What are you doing to ensure that this is kept under control?

You might find it helpful to re-read what you wrote for Activity 31 in answering this final point.

Reflect and review

 1 Reflect and review

Now that you have completed your work on *Managing the Employment Relationship,* let us review each of our unit objectives.

You should be **better able to**:

■ define 'diversity' and explain why it is important to manage diversity at work.

We have stressed how, unless diversity at work is actively pursued, there cannot be real harmony and full use cannot be made of everyone's abilities. We have also seen how some groups – especially women, racial minorities and the disabled – suffer from lack of equal treatment and opportunity at work. We have also examined many of the ways in which the law on equality can be broken at work. You should feel that you have a better appreciation of the problems and the unfairness of many practices and systems in the workplace, and you should be able to explain to your colleagues why diversity is important.

You may want to ask yourself the following questions regarding these points.

■ Have I read and understood my organization's policy on equal opportunities?

_____

_____

_____

■ Do I understand why diversity at work is important?

_____

_____

_____

- Do I understand how certain practices in the workplace can cause some groups to suffer from lack of equal treatment?

_____

_____

_____

The second workbook objective was as follows.

- Outline the main legislation relating to fair employment.

You should understand the principles of the statute law and other regulations, the main types of discrimination made illegal under them and the forms which that discrimination can take. You should also appreciate the way in which the law is evolving.

You may want to ask yourself the following questions.

Am I confident that I can apply the principles of the law to ensure that all my team are treated legally within it?

_____

_____

_____

Can I see how procedures and customs may have to change to meet the new requirements if and when they become law?

_____

_____

_____

Do I understand that the law **cannot** change attitudes or how people think, but **can** demand that they behave in accordance with its provisions?

_____

_____

_____

The next workbook objective was as follows.

- Recognize whether the law has been broken.

The five-point checklist should have helped you in achieving this objective. The checklist was designed to help you decide whether any inequality of treatment is breaking the law on discrimination. It should be useful in achieving good personnel practices at work. You should now feel that you know how to find out if anything unlawful could occur or has occurred, and know what to do to prevent unlawful discrimination taking place. It is worth bearing in mind the fact that you will be individually liable for: any acts you commit yourself; any instruction you give others to commit; any pressure you put on others to commit; and any you knowingly help others to commit. Remember too that if you are negligent you can increase the likelihood of your employer sharing liability for individual acts of discrimination.

You might find these questions useful.

■ Do I use only relevant factors for selection?

_____

_____

_____

■ Do I make sure that proper records are kept of the reasons behind important decisions?

_____

_____

_____

■ Have I explained to everyone in my work team the main points of the law in regard to equality at work?

_____

_____

_____

The next objective was:

■ Understand and implement your organization's employment policies and procedures as a major step towards managing your team fairly and consistently within the law.

Employment procedures and policies translate the principles and the developing practice of the law into day-to-day rules and procedures which all managers must implement.

The law itself is evolving continuously and managers rely on senior and specialist managers in their organizations to keep their procedures up to date with essential changes, taking advice from external sources such as ACAS.

■ Are you confident that you know your own organization's procedures sufficiently thoroughly?

_____

■ In practice, do you follow the procedures implicitly, or are there barriers which you need to surmount, personally or with help from your own manager?

_____

_____

The next objective was to be able to:

■ describe the steps you **can** take to ensure diversity in the workplace.

Keeping within the law is only a starting point. Your aim should be to build up the kind of atmosphere in your workplace whereby everyone is committed to achieving full equality of treatment and opportunity for all. This requires you to lead by example, to be open-minded when dealing with issues of equality and to work at avoiding stereotypical ways of thinking about specific groups of people.

Some questions you might like to ask yourself are as follows.

■ Can I honestly say that, if any incident of unjustifiable discrimination took place in my workgroup, I would be aware of it?

_____

_____

_____

■ Do I know the views of my workgroup on the subject of equality at work?

_____

_____

_____

■ What steps do I take to ensure that I am open to complaints or suggestions about the way members of my work team are treated at work?

_____

_____

_____

The next objective was to be able to:

■ describe the consequences of non-compliance for your own work area and organization.

You may want to think about the following points.

Do I know what my responsibilities are for my own working area and what could happen if I fail to meet them?

_____

_____

_____

Do I appreciate the nature and the levels of sanctions which an Employment Tribunal can impose and the financial, organizational and personnel implications of them?

_____

_____

_____

Can I now plan to ensure that adverse consequences do not arise from those aspects of potential illegal discrimination which I can control directly, or influence through my manager or specialist managers, for example in the human resources department?

_____

_____

_____

_____

_____

_____

The final objective was:

■ Deal with disciplinary matters in a fair and consistent way within the law.

Taking formal disciplinary action is a sensitive and difficult process to instigate, especially when it involves people with whom you work every day and on whom you rely to give you support.

It often requires a great deal of moral fibre to act when it would be easy to look the other way – especially where employees have developed their own ways of doing things, which, though against the rules, have become established custom and practice.

Nevertheless, if some employees are allowed to get away with poor standards of performance or conduct, morale will suffer among their peers, or general standards will decline. The disciplinary procedures described, based on ACAS guidance and accepted as fair by the law and by independent trades unions, are there to provide an impersonal, consistent way to bring those who can't, or won't for the time being, meet the standards required back into line with them.

■ Are you confident that you know your own organization's procedures sufficiently well and are prepared to apply them without fear or favour?

_____

■ Are there aspects of the procedures you know insufficiently well, or lack confidence to enact? If so, what plans do you have to address the issues?

_____

_____

2 Action plan

Use this plan to develop further for yourself a course of action you want to take. Make a note in the left-hand column of the issues or problems you want to tackle, and then decide what you intend to do, and make a note in column 2.

The resources you need might include time, materials, information or money. You may need to negotiate for some of them, but they could be something easily acquired, like half an hour of somebody's time, or a chapter of a book. Put whatever you need in column 3. No plan means anything without a timescale, so put a realistic target completion date in column 4.

Finally, describe the outcome you want to achieve as a result of this plan, whether it is for your own benefit or advancement, or a more efficient way of doing things.

Desired outcomes					
	1 Issues	2 Action	3 Resources	4 Target completion	
Actual outcomes					

3 Extensions

Extension 1

The Equal Opportunities Commission, the Commission for Racial Equality and the Disability Rights Commission.

The Equal Opportunities Commission
Overseas House
Quay Street
Manchester M3 3HN
www.eoc.org.uk
Telephone helpline: 0845 601 5901

The Commission for Racial Equality
Elliot House
10–12 Allington Street
London SW1 5EH
www.cre.org.uk
Telephone: 020 7828 7022

The Disability Rights Commission
DRC Helpline
Freepost MID 02164
Stratford-upon-Avon
CV37 9HY
www.drc-gb.org
Telephone 0845 762 2633

From 2007 these three are due to merge, to form the Commission for Equality and Human Rights (CEHR).

■ Their tasks are to:

- help eliminate discrimination;
- promote equality of opportunity;
- keep the law relating to equality under review, and to propose amendments.

■ Each Commission has published a Code of Practice (see Extension 4).

■ The Commissions can:

- formally investigate particular industries, or practices, or issues;
- help an individual bring a case;
- provide legal aid to an individual.

Each Commission must make a Formal Investigation before it can use its powers of enforcement. This will usually call for information to be disclosed by the organization it is investigating. Suppressing or destroying documents, or refusing to attend to give evidence, can result in a heavy fine.

- A Commission can take legal action against those who discriminate in advertising for jobs, or who help or put pressure on others to discriminate.

- A Commission can issue Non-Discrimination Notices if it finds evidence of unlawful discrimination. A Notice lasts five years and will require that discrimination stops, that practices are changed to achieve this, that everyone is told about the practices, and that information is kept available about the actions taken.

- A Commission can also get an injunction against employers and individuals who discriminate or are likely to do so. An injunction is enforceable as contempt of court.

- An individual with a complaint about discrimination can get certain kinds of help from the relevant Commission. He or she can also take a case to an Employment Tribunal. The Tribunal has powers to: award compensation (there is no upper limit on the amount which can be awarded); recommend the employer takes action on discrimination; and/or order reinstatement if the individual has been dismissed.

  Compensation can be for:

  - actual or future loss of wages and benefits;
  - injury to feelings.

- Cases must usually be brought within three months of the event complained of, although applications to tribunals under the Equal Pay Act can be made at any time during the employment in question and up to six months afterwards.

  The person making the complaint must prove his or her case and can ask the employer to fill in a questionnaire which provides information that would otherwise be unavailable to the complainant. If the employer fails to fill in the questionnaire, this will probably tell against it in the eyes of the Tribunal.

  To find out more about the law in action, you might consider attending an Employment Tribunal yourself. You can telephone the Commissions and ask when the next case relating to equality is to be heard, and where it will take place. You may find there are not many cases, but when one does come up it will be of great value and interest for you to attend.

Reflect and review

Extension 2   Book   *The Disability Discrimination Act 1995 – What Employers Need to Know*
Edition   April 1999
Publisher   Disability Rights Commission
www.drc.gb.org

Extension 3   Useful codes of practice and guides.

The five-point checklist given in Session C is based on recommendations that you will find in greater detail in two clear and excellent practical guides:

■ *The Race Relations Code of Practice* published by the Commission for Racial Equality;
■ *The Equal Opportunities Code of Practice* published by the Equal Opportunities Commission.

The Codes do not impose any new legal obligations, and like this workbook, neither is an authoritative statement of the law. However, if the steps the Codes recommend are followed in the workplace, then it is most unlikely that unlawful discrimination will occur. Even if an individual commits an unlawful act, if the employer can show, particularly by reference to records, that the steps recommended have been:

■ established;
■ known and understood throughout the organization; and
■ followed in all but exceptional cases,

then the employer will almost certainly not carry liability for such exceptional cases.

There are also two very thorough guides prepared by the Home Office and available free of charge from local job centres and ACAS (Advisory Conciliation and Arbitration Service) offices.

■ *Sex Discrimination: A guide to the Sex Discrimination Act, 1975.*
■ *Racial Discrimination: A guide to the Race Relations Act, 1976.*

The TUC workbooks on *Tackling Racism* and *Working Women* are excellent and well-produced booklets. They are full of practical illustrations, real incidents and brief 'activities' that will enable you to extend even further your understanding of, and ability to do something positive about, inequality at work.

The *Code of Good Practice on the Employment of Disabled People*, promoted by the Department for Education and Employment is also available.

Here is the five-point checklist in more detail.

1   **Relevant factors** are the only ones which should be taken into account when making decisions at work.

These factors should:	They should **not**:
■ be clear and unambiguous; ■ be measurable if possible.	■ be based on personal bias; ■ lead to discrimination.

These factors should:	They should **not**:

Relevant factors might be:	**Irrelevant** factors might be:
■ skills and knowledge in the job; ■ experience of the work; ■ good references; ■ job history; ■ appearance and personality; ■ amount of effort put in.	■ skills in English; ■ the sex of the applicant; ■ disability; ■ colour of skin; ■ age; ■ ethnic origins.

2   There should be **procedures** to ensure that there is objectivity and equality of treatment.

The procedures should be:	They should **not** be:
■ clearly defined; ■ understood by everyone; ■ agreed by management; ■ written down and available for everyone to read.	■ able to be interpreted in such a way as to allow bias and prejudice to creep in; ■ difficult to follow.

3   **Training and guidance** should be given in these procedures to everyone who has to carry them out, and to everyone who will be affected by them.

The training and guidance should be:

■ available to all who use it and need it;
■ given by people with a thorough knowledge of the subject and feeling for it, with the ability to transmit those ideas;
■ given as frequently as needed;
■ checked to make sure it is effective.

4   **Checks** on policy, procedures and practice should take place regularly. Corrective **action** must be taken where checks show it to be necessary.

The checks should:

- show whether a process is working well (validity);
- show whether it achieves the same results no matter who uses it; when, or in what situation (reliability);
- provide monitoring and analysis to show the sex and racial origins of the workforce and of job applicants to discover whether there has been equality of treatment and opportunity;
- have their purpose and operation explained to everyone;
- ensure that there is adequate confidentiality of information;
- result in discipline for those who show discriminatory behaviour, or behaviour which is likely to encourage or lead to discrimination;
- result in corrective action when problems are shown up.

Problems may mean that women or people from racial minorities, or disabled people:

- tend not to apply for employment or promotion;
- tend not to get recruited or promoted;
- are under-represented in training, or in jobs carrying higher pay, status or authority;
- are concentrated in certain shifts, sections, workgroups or departments.

5 **Records** must be kept to prove that all reasonable practical steps have been taken to achieve equality of treatment. Those records should:

- enable anyone to find out exactly what procedures exist, and what is happening in every personnel process;
- enable anyone to measure how successful the organization's equal opportunity policy is;
- show the reasons for the selection or rejection of each individual in every selection decision (assuming that this is not too time-consuming or expensive);
- provide up-to-date and comprehensive records of the sex, marital and ethnic composition of the workforce;
- show that all reasonable and practical steps have been taken to achieve equality in the workplace;
- show the procedures, training and guidance given, checks carried out and corrective action.

Extension 4   Equal opportunity policy statement.

Here is an example of a county council's equal opportunity policy statement. It contains reference to procedures that the council will establish and review, to ensure that the policy is carried out.

Equal opportunities policy

The County Council accepts that problems of discrimination are encountered by certain groups and minorities in the field of employment. In order to reflect both the Authority's concern and commitment to ensuring that no policies or procedures in the organization operate to the detriment of any group, it has adopted a formal approach to the field of equal opportunities.

The Authority's policy was formulated with due regard to the guidelines issued by the Commission for Racial Equality and the Equal Opportunities Commission and with the co-operation and assistance of the trade unions.

The responsibility for ensuring non-discriminatory practices lies not only with the employers but with all members of staff.

Policy statement

This County Council believes in equal opportunities in all circumstances. As an employer the aim of the policy is to ensure that no job applicant or employee receives less favourable treatment on the grounds of sex, colour, ethnic or national origins, marital status, domestic circumstances, sexual orientation, trade union activity, political or religious belief or is disadvantaged by conditions or requirements which cannot be shown to be justifiable. Selection criteria and procedures will be frequently reviewed to ensure that individuals are selected, promoted and treated on the basis of their relative merits and abilities. All employees will be given equal opportunity and, where appropriate, special training to progress within the organization. This policy applies to the disabled who have the necessary attributes for the job.

This Authority is committed to a programme of action to make this policy fully effective.

Monitoring

To provide a factual basis for consideration and review of recruitment and employment policies, all job applicants are now asked to voluntarily complete a confidential monitoring sheet. In order to assess the Authority's present position a staff audit will be made in the near future. Again, this will be done on a confidential voluntary basis.

Extension 5

Booklet	*Contracts of employment*
Edition	February 2002
Publisher	ACAS

Extension 6	Booklet	*Varying a contract of employment*
	Edition	July 2000
	Publisher	ACAS

Extension 7 — ACAS produces various leaflets to help you manage effectively within the law.

You can get more information by visiting www.acas.org.uk

Extension 8	Book	*Bullying and Harassment at Work – Managers/Employers*
	Edition	November 1999
	Publisher	ACAS

Extension 9	Book	*Disciplinary and Grievance Procedures*
	Edition	September 2000
	Publisher	ACAS

Extension 10	Book	*Producing Disciplinary and Grievance Procedures*
	Edition	November 2001
	Publisher	ACAS

Extension 11	Book	*Producing a Written Statement*
	Edition	November 2001
	Publisher	ACAS

Extension 12	Book	*Representation at Work*
	Edition	January 2002
	Publisher	ACAS

4 Answers to self-assessment questions

Self-assessment 1 on page 11

1 People in the workplace may be discriminated against because of race, religion, gender, sexual orientation, age, cultural origins, mental or physical disability.

2 Equality of treatment and **OPPORTUNITY** is important:

- to encourage good **RELATIONSHIPS** in the workplace and
- to make the best use of everyone's **ABILITIES**.

3   Inequality occurs when a person or **GROUP** is **UNJUSTIFIABLY** treated in a less **FAVOURABLE** way than another is, or would be, treated in the same sort of situation.

4   The four-point checklist.

    a   What are the **FACTS**?
    b   Is there any difference in **TREATMENT**?
    c   Does anyone suffer any **DISADVANTAGE**?
    d   Does any **JUSTIFICATION** exist?

5   The statement that 'Equality means everyone has the same abilities and opportunities.' is **FALSE**. The other statements are **TRUE**.

Self-assessment 2 on pages 38–40

1   The law relating to unfair discrimination sets out to **BAN/OUTLAW** such practices on a number of specified **GROUNDS** to **PROTECT** members of groups whom it defines as having been **DISADVANTAGED** previously at work.

2   The eight grounds on which discrimination can be unlawful are:

sex; nationality; marital status; ethnic origin; race; national origin; colour; disability.

3   **DIRECT** discrimination occurs when someone is treated less favourably than others are, or would be, directly on grounds of sex, marital status, race, colour, nationality, ethnic or national origins, disability.

INDIRECT discrimination means setting conditions for employment which are unnecessary, and which have the effect of preventing certain groups from being appointed.

4   Discrimination is justifiable where it is carried out because of the need for a **GENUINE OCCUPATIONAL QUALIFICATION**.

5   The offence of '**INSTRUCTION** to discriminate' can only be committed when an order to discriminate is given by someone who is in a position to do so.

6   The Disability Discrimination Act requires employers to make **REASONABLE ADJUSTMENT** to help disabled employees, which treat each **CASE** on its' own **MERITS**.

7   a   One group tries to put pressure on another to discriminate unlawfully, but the unlawful discrimination does not take place.

    This **IS** an offence in all but cases under the Disability Discrimination Act 1995. The correct name for it is **PRESSURE TO DISCRIMINATE**.

b A group of workers is made up of members from two different countries. There are one or two arguments, so the supervisor separates them and makes them work as separate racial groups.

This **IS** an offence. The correct name for it is **SEGREGATION**.

c Someone is accused of unlawful discrimination, but says that he was merely obeying an order from his manager, although he didn't agree with it.

This **IS** an offence. The correct name for the manager's offence is **INSTRUCTION TO DISCRIMINATE**. The employee is still guilty of discrimination.

d An employee accuses his workmates of unlawful discrimination. They are very angry and respond by 'sending him to Coventry'.

This **IS** an offence. The correct name for it is **VICTIMIZATION**.

8 Recent legislation which could be relevant to illegal discriminatory practices at work, includes:
European Human Rights Legislation; Parental leave; Working Time Directive; Public Interest Disclosure Act.

9 Other areas of working life which are being looked at include defining unfair discrimination on the basis of **AGE**, **RELIGION** or **SEXUAL ORIENTATION**.

10 The Public Interest Disclosure act, commonly known as the '**WHISTLE-BLOWING**' Act, **PROTECTS** employees who report a wide range of **GENUINE CONCERNS** about employment practices.

11 The best way to stay within the law is to manage within both its **LETTER** and **SPIRIT** and to develop **CONTINGENCY** plans to **ANTICIPATE** other **EMPLOYMENT** practices which may break it. It is all part of a modern manager's job.

Self-assessment 3 on page 64

1 Anyone who knowingly aids another to commit an **UNLAWFUL** act of discrimination will share **LIABILITY** for that act.

2 **VICARIOUS** liability simply means whoever is finally responsible for individuals who commit unlawful acts also has responsibility for those acts.

3 The employer as well as the individual employee is liable for any unlawful act of discrimination committed by the employee unless it is shown that the

employer has taken all **REASONABLE PRACTICAL STEPS** to prevent discrimination occurring.

4   The five-point checklist is as follows.

    a Identify the relevant **FACTORS**.
    b Install the **PROCEDURES**.
    c Provide the **TRAINING** and guidance.
    d Carry out regular **CHECKS**.
    e Maintain the **RECORDS**.

5   The statement 'A team leader is always responsible for any act of unlawful discrimination by a member of his or her team.' is **FALSE**. If the team leader was unaware of the discrimination and did not condone it, he or she would not normally be held responsible. The other two statements are **TRUE**.

Self-assessment 4 on pages 78–9

1   The law impinges on many aspects of employing people, including contracts of employment, equal opportunities, data protection, trade unions, and health, safety and welfare at work.

2   Three ways in which an employer can ensure that its employment policies are communicated effectively to all employees are: providing an employee handbook; providing induction training; and giving regular briefings.

3   **Unfair dismissal, discrimination in regard to race, sex or disability** and **victimization** are three of the main grounds on which an employee can make an application to an Employment Tribunal.

4   Well established grievance procedures help an organization to manage legally by giving employees the chance to raise issues which concern them in a formal way, with built-in safeguards and appeals to independent managers.

5   The main stages in a formal disciplinary procedure as recommended by ACAS are:

    1 recorded verbal warning;
    2 first written warning;
    3 final written warning;
    4 dismissal.

6   An important principle of sound disciplinary procedures is that **no manager** is allowed to dismiss their **immediate** subordinate without reference to a higher level of management.

7 No matter how good a disciplinary procedure is, it will not be effective legally unless it is applied **fairly** and **consistently**.

8 Written records of disciplinary procedures used concerning an individual employee are essential to prove to an **Employment Tribunal** that an organization has acted fairly.

9 Appeal procedures are an essential part of **disciplinary** procedures if they are to be seen as fair by an **Employment Tribunal**.

10 The membership of an employment tribunal comprises a 'chair' who is legally qualified, a second member with **commercial experience** and a third who has a **practical trade union** background.

Self-assessment 5 on pages 100–1

1 Employees who believe they have been **ILLEGALLY DISCRIMINATED** against can apply to an **EMPLOYMENT TRIBUNAL** without serving any **QUALIFYING** period.

2 Four potential adverse consequences of reinstatement are as follows.

■ For the organization – deciding what to do with the person who replaced the reinstated one.
■ For the team leader whose area is affected – personal humiliation.
■ For the other team members – difficulty re-adjusting to their former colleague.
■ For the person reinstated – being made to feel unwelcome by former colleagues.

3 Tribunals can make **ADDITIONAL** awards in respect of **HURT FEELINGS**, in addition to those made for direct loss wages, salary or financial benefits.

4 Four examples of practices which might be seen as bullying or harassment are as follows.

■ Unwanted advances to members of the opposite sex.
■ Using nicknames based on physical disability.
■ Making jokes about someone's race.
■ Physical intimidation for any reason.

5 The consequences for a team leader complicit in acts of illegal discrimination could include **LOSS** of **RESPECT** from team members, **DISCIPLINARY ACTION** or loss of **PROMOTIONAL** opportunities.

6   **STEREOTYPING** of roles can lead to claims of **ILLEGAL** discrimination from members of groups who feel **EXCLUDED/PRECLUDED** from applying for them.

7   Word of mouth recruitment is an example of a recruitment practice which is likely to be seen as **AUTOMATICALLY/ILLEGALLY DISCRIMINATORY**.

8   Employment Tribunals are under no obligation to consider the **ABILITY** of **ORGANIZATIONS** to **PAY** the compensation which they award.

9   The consequences for a company found guilty of illegal discrimination can include loss of **REPUTATION** and customer **GOODWILL** as well as any direct financial penalties.

10   To convince an Employment Tribunal of your case you must be able to **PROVE** that on the **BALANCE** of **PROBABILITIES** the decision which you took is justified.

11   Three things which, if mishandled by a local team leader, could lead to serious consequences under the legislation are:

- workplace stress;
- harassment and bullying;
- family friendly policies.

Self-assessment 6 on pages 138–9

1   All disciplinary offences involve a **breach of the rules**.

2   If a disciplinary offence is minor, a first line manager might decide that, rather than beginning the formal disciplinary procedure, they should have an **informal discussion** with the team member.

3   **Everybody involved** benefits from there being clear rules for dealing with disciplinary offences.

4   Here are the actions you might take, set out in order.

   e   Decide who should be present.
   b   Decide where the meeting is to be held.
   f   Introduce the participants, and state why they are there.
   i   Give the employee a chance to state his or her case.
   a   Decide what penalty should be imposed.
   h   Sum up what's been said.
   d   Continue to monitor performance.

▪ 5 Answers to activities

Activity 12 on page 25

Examples of unfair discrimination affected by Directives are as follows.

1 Human Rights. This legislation casts its net so widely that it could impact on almost any aspect of anti-discrimination law. For example:

- an employee being investigated for alleged discriminatory behaviour might claim that using video surveillance techniques prejudiced the right to privacy;
- an employee who has unsuccessfully pursued a grievance alleging discrimination through standard procedures might claim that failure to resolve it satisfactorily was an infringement of human rights.

2 Working Time. In some industries, long working hours are common. If these hours are more commonly associated with one sex, or with workers from one ethnic group, this could lead to claims of unfair discrimination.

3 Minimum Wage. In industries where piece work is common, pressure could arise claiming that this discriminates against lower-paid workers of one sex or ethnic group, especially if piece work targets are hard to meet and such work is predominately done by one sex or the other.

4 Ageism. If your employer makes a point of employing people over the age of, say, 45, in some jobs, this could fall foul of any legislation brought in. So could advertising for a trainee worker, specifying **any** age limits or job advertisements quoting a maximum age for applicants.

Activity 14 on page 30

1 The Sex Discrimination and Race Relations Act both outlaw unfair discrimination on the grounds of **RECRUITMENT** and **SELECTION** for employment.

2 Under the Disability Discrimination Act, an employee who suffered a **TEMPORARY** incapacity following a skiing accident would **NOT** be protected.

3 Under the Equal Pay Act, **MEN** and **WOMEN** must be paid **EQUALLY** for doing the **SAME** work or work assessed as being of **EQUAL** value.

4 It is illegal to dismiss a **PREGNANT** employee solely on the grounds of pregnancy.

5   Victimization is banned under both the **SEX DISCRIMINATION** Act and the **RACE RELATIONS** Act.

6   Disability is defined as a **PHYSICAL** or **MENTAL** impairment which has a **SUBSTANTIAL** and long-term **ADVERSE** effect.

7   Time off for **ANTE-NATAL** care is a legal right for a pregnant employee as is **RETURN** to **WORK** after maternity leave.

Activity 22 on page 46

The areas of personnel you've listed may be included in the following list.

- Recruitment
- Selection
- Promotion
- Transfer
- Induction
- Health and Safety
- Pay
- Working conditions
- Appraisal
- Training
- Dismissal
- Redundancy

Activity 54 on page 116

If you glance back through the procedure, you will see that the correct answers are:

1   Would every minor offence have to be taken through the procedure above? No: as is stated at the start, minor faults are dealt with informally.

2   In which stages do the warnings given become spent or are disregarded after a certain period of time? Stages 1, 2 and 3.

3   After which stages does the employee have a right of appeal? **All** stages.

4   At which stages are the warnings written down? **All** stages.

5   At which stages does the employee receive a written document? Stages 2, 3 and 4.

Reflect and review

Activity 57 on pages 119–20

I Mrs Jones in the wages department

It might be difficult convincing someone that this was a disciplinary offence. Some of the reasons are that:

- her office first line manager knew what was going on;
- she took as little time as possible – using some of her coffee break;
- other people had done the same thing, so there was a precedent;
- her personal circumstances provided a good reason why she wanted to make the collection;
- she made sure her work was done.

2 Mrs Jones in the reception area

You may agree that her behaviour warrants some form of disciplinary action. Some of the reasons you may have put down are that:

- there is no evidence that she asked anyone's permission;
- she spent a long time on the collection;
- she had already been warned about her behaviour;
- the collection could almost be considered as being for her own benefit;
- it is part of her job to be in a specific place. In this case, it is important that somebody is there to meet visitors at reception.

If you agreed with my arguments, perhaps you will also agree that these two cases contrasted dramatically. One was clearly not an offence, while the other clearly was. If you have had experience of dealing with disciplinary matters, you will know that decisions are often much more difficult than this.

Activity 62 on page 132

The only answer to this question is: the procedure of the organization where you work.

If there is no agreed procedure, you could follow the example procedure given by ACAS as outlined in Session C. Obviously, any previous offences still on record involving the **same individual** may well affect your decision. Don't forget also that any previous cases involving **different** individuals but the **same offence** should be taken into account: the aim is consistency.

Activity 64 on pages 133–4

You may have noticed a number of ways in which this ending of the interview is an improvement on our last example. The first line manager:

- stated what the offence was;
- gave Ray a chance to comment;

- gave the trade union representative the chance to comment;
- told Ray about the company's disciplinary procedure, and what a further offence might lead to;
- told Ray about his right of appeal;
- told Ray that the offence could be erased from the records after six months;
- made clear, unambiguous statements.

⬛ 6 Answers to the quick quiz

Answer 1   Diversity needs to be managed to ensure that people with different characteristics are treated equally.

Answer 2   The important missing word is **unjustifiably**. 'Inequality at work occurs when a person or group is **unjustifiably** treated in a less favourable way than others in the same situation.'

Answer 3   The first thing you should do is find out all the facts.

Answer 4   Since nobody has suffered any disadvantage it is unlikely that an offence has been committed.

Answer 5   The Act is designed to prevent discrimination against **either** sex.

Answer 6   **Direct discrimination** occurs when someone is treated less favourably than others are, or would be, directly on grounds of sex, marriage, disability, race, colour, nationality, ethnic or national origins.

Answer 7   **Indirect discrimination** means setting conditions for employment which are unnecessary and which have the effect of preventing certain groups from being appointed.

Answer 8   The letters **GOQ** stand for 'genuine occupational qualification'.

Answer 9   **Victimization**, in this context, means treating someone unfavourably because they have, truthfully and in good faith, reported or alleged unlawful discrimination or given information or evidence in a discrimination case.

Answer 10   If you obey an instruction to discriminate unfairly then you are liable in law.

Answer 11   Your answer should say, in your own words, that **positive action** means giving certain groups extra help to catch up with the experience and qualifications of others. It is not allowed in respect of recruitment, selection or promotion.

Answer 12   An employer has to have taken all reasonable practical steps to prevent unlawful discrimination.

Answer 13   Records are important because, in case of dispute, the employer must be able to prove that he has taken all reasonable practical steps.

Answer 14   You should have mentioned two of the following points.

- Installing procedures to ensure there is objectivity and equality of treatment.
- Giving training and guidance on these procedures.
- Carrying out checks on policy, procedures and practice.
- Keeping accurate records.

Answer 15   A **stereotype** is a standardized, oversimplified mental picture of some group such as the idea that all women like babies or all men know how to mend an engine.

Answer 16   Equality concerns everybody, not just the specific groups listed.

Answer 17   There is no upper limit in such cases – payments have exceeded £1 million.

Answer 18   **Reinstatement** is being re-employed in the former occupation, as though you had never left it, retaining all former remuneration rights and conditions of service. **Re-employment** is being taken back into a job which may be at a lower level of pay and inferior conditions of service.

Answer 19   Discrimination on the basis of **AGE, RELIGIOUS BELIEF** and **SEXUAL ORIENTATION** are being considered as additional aspects of illegal discrimination.

Answer 20   The statement is **FALSE**. There is no service qualification period.

Answer 21   Things that a first line manager could control or influence include bullying; sexual harassment; informal means of recruitment; workplace stress; flexible working arrangements; family-friendly policies and use of an appraisal system.

Answer 22   Two of the most important documents employees should normally expect to have to conform with the employment laws are the contract of employment and a written statement of terms and conditions of employment.

Answer 23   Some of the steps which the law may expect an employer to take are: providing proper induction training, helping employees whose first language is not English, and explaining intelligibly the meaning of expressions such as 'gross misconduct'.

Answer 24 Apart from gross misconduct, three ways in which employees might break their contract of employment are: by failing to meet reasonable performance targets, by being late for work, and by failing to observe the procedure for reporting in when absent through sickness.

Answer 25 Employees who believe that they have been dismissed unfairly can apply to an Employment Tribunal to have their case against the former employer heard.

Answer 26 A recognized trade union will be able to represent a member's interests during disciplinary hearings and appeals procedures.

Answer 27 The existence of an appeals procedure in grievance procedures ensures that the employee can take their concerns to a manager who will be reasonably detached from the employee's immediate situation, and whose personal prejudices cannot cloud the issue.

Answer 28 The letters 'ACAS' are an abbreviation for the Advisory, Conciliation and Arbitration Service.

Answer 29 Maintaining accurate, up-to-date records is important because:

- legal proceedings may start some time after the events referred to;
- people's memories are unreliable;
- people don't always tell the truth;
- the records will provide concrete evidence that procedures were followed to the letter.

Answer 30 Discipline at work has the four main objectives of: safety; prosperity of the organization; fairness; compliance with a contract.

Answer 31 Stage 1: oral warning. Stage 2 – Written warning. Stage 3 – Final written warning or disciplinary suspension. Stage 4 – Dismissal.

Answer 32 ACAS suggest that gross misconduct includes: theft, fraud or deliberate falsification of records; fighting, or assault on another person; deliberate damage to company property; serious incapability through alcohol or being under the influence of illegal drugs; serious negligence which causes unacceptable loss, damage or injury; serious acts of insubordination.

Answer 33 We said that the purposes of a disciplinary interview are to:

- allow the employee to give his or her version of the incident;
- ensure a full discussion, so that everyone present has a chance to hear the facts and to present any new facts;
- advise the employee of his or her rights;
- enable a fair judgement to be made so that an appropriate penalty can be awarded.

● 7 Certificate

Completion of this certificate by an authorized person shows that you have worked through all the parts of this workbook and satisfactorily completed the assessments. The certificate provides a record of what you have done that may be used for exemptions or as evidence of prior learning against other nationally certificated qualifications.

superseries

Managing the Employment Relationship

....

has satisfactorily completed this workbook

Name of signatory ....

Position ....

Signature ....

Date ....

Official stamp

Pergamon
Flexible
Learning

Fifth Edition

superseries

FIFTH EDITION

Workbooks in the series:

For prices and availability please telephone our order helpline
or email

+44 (0) 1865 474010
directorders@elsevier.com